ARE YOU LOST IN YOUR SH*T?

A PERSONAL GUIDE TO CONQUERING YOUR INNER STRUGGLES AND DISCOVERING A BETTER YOU

SIMON COCKRAM

ARE YOU LOST IN YOUR SH*T?

A Personal Guide to Conquering Your Inner Struggles and Discovering a Better You

By Simon Cockram

Copyright © 2024 Simon Cockram. All rights reserved.

This work depicts actual events in the life of the author as truthfully as recollection permits. While all persons and businesses within are real, names and identifying characteristics may have been changed to respect privacy.

No part of this publication may be reproduced, stored in a retrieval system, or transmitted in any form or by any means, electronic, mechanical, photocopying, recording, scanning, or otherwise, without the prior written permission of the publisher.

Limit of Liability/Disclaimer of Warranty: The information presented in this book is for educational and informational purposes only. It is not intended to be a substitute for professional advice or treatment. Never disregard or delay seeking professional advice because of something you have read in this book. The author and publisher are not licensed therapists, and the content provided is based on personal experiences, research, and opinions. The author and publisher make no representations or warranties, express or implied, regarding the accuracy, completeness, or usefulness of the information contained in this book. To the fullest extent permitted by law, the author and publisher disclaim any liability for any loss, damage, or injury that may occur from the use or misuse of this book, or any other materials provided in connection with this book.

Book cover design by Saqib Arshad

Printed in the United States of America

DEDICATION

For my son and soon-to-be-born baby, I hope everything I've learned will help give you the best possible start in life. I want you to know that you are enough, deeply loved, beautiful souls, and perfect just as you are.

To my wife: Your unwavering support over the past decade has helped me become the man I always aspired to be. Words will never do justice to my love and gratitude for you. Thank you for the joy and love you bring into each day. I love you beyond measure.

CONTENTS

ARE YOU LOST IN YOUR SHIT!?	1
YOUR LIFE	3
SECTION 01 - YOUR MIND	7
CHAPTER 1: WHY DID YOU PICK THIS BOOK UP?	9
Let's be mates	13
Tell me about you	15
Why is Journaling Important?	17
Your past, present, and future	20
Chapter 1 Summary	24
CHAPTER 2: INTRODUCTION TO MASLOW'S HIERARCHY OF HUMAN NEEDS	27
CHAPTER 3: THE BIG PROBLEM	33
The Abyss	35
What is the Abyss?	37
The role of dopamine and your habits	39
The Mind	41
The wonderful Amy Winehouse	43
Let's return to your childhood and find the root causes of your emotional discomfort	45
Professional support	47
Your Inner child	50
Rapid Transformational Therapy (RTT)	52
Chapter 3 summary	54
CHAPTER 3: YOUR HABIT CYCLES	57
Negative habits	59
Finding a better way to respond	62
Are you Surviving or Thriving?	67
The Desired State	69
Initial Discomfort and Resistance	71

CHAPTER 5: WHAT'S HOLDING YOU BACK FROM FEELING YOUR BEST?   75

Ultra-processed Junk Food and Sugar   75
Alcohol   78
Eating or drinking your emotions   80
Tobacco and Nicotine   83
Recreational Drugs   86
Life's paradoxes   89
One day at a time   91
Summary of Your Mind   93

SECTION 02 - YOUR BODY   95

The Mirror and The Market   98
The health risk to you   100
Your Body and You   102

CHAPTER 7: SLEEP   105

The Foundation of a Better Body: Sleep   105
The Critical Role of Circadian Rhythm   106
How to Lose Weight   108
Please never go on a 'diet' ever again   113
Body Composition   116
The Importance of Cardiovascular Exercise   119
Learning to love exercise   121
The crucial role of flow state   124
Why Health and Fitness is rented   128
Investing in a Personal Trainer: Your Guide to Lasting Fitness Success   130
Summary of Your Body   133

SECTION 03 - YOUR MONEY   135

CHAPTER 8: MONEY IS FREEDOM   137

The Quiet Strength of True Wealth   139
The Richest Man in Babylon   141
An Introduction to Investing   143
Compound interest   146
What are Low-cost ETFs?   148
Your Money   151
Your Expenses   155
A Reflection on Money, Time, and Choices   159

CHAPTER 9: YOUR SOUL — 163

- Another Look into Meditation — 166
- How to Meditate — 169
- Introducing Ikigai — 171
- Your Motivation — 174
- Law of Attraction and Consistent Action — 177
- 10,000 hours to become a Master — 183
- Purpose, Passion or Your Life's Task — 186
- Transcendence: Expanding Maslow's Vision — 189
- Help who you were — 194

THE FINAL CHAPTER: YOUR ESCAPE — 197
THANK YOU — 199

ARE YOU LOST IN YOUR SHIT!?

Thank you for your curiosity about this book's title and contents. Maybe, you laughed at the question, *"Are you lost in your shit?"* and answered 'yes' with a smile, or perhaps a friend bought it for you, which is either a joke, an insult, or them trying to try to help you, genuinely. Either way, something resonated, and here we are.

Reading this book is the first step toward feeling better, less lost, and less overwhelmed. It's the beginning of reducing anxiety, escaping constant overthinking, and, most importantly, finding a clear path to living life to its fullest potential.

By the end of this book, we will have embarked on a deep, introspective journey that I promise will be **life-changing for you**.

A Surprising Truth: Did you know that around 85% of people will buy at least one self-help book in their lifetime, yet only 10% make it to the last page? Even fewer, less than 5%, apply what they've learned. By committing to read and act on the insights in these pages, you're already setting yourself apart and taking a decisive step toward fundamental transformation. Don't let this be just another book collecting dust; let this be the one that truly changes your life.

A Decision Point: You now have a choice. Do you genuinely want to live your best life, or do you want to continue feeling low, lost, and unfulfilled? How long are you willing to stay stuck?

If you answer yes, I invite you to move forward, read this book, and actively engage with the process.

What This Book Offers: This book is about making simple, daily choices that improve your behaviour, build positive habits, and inspire action. When compounded over time, these small steps can remarkably impact your life.

A Commitment to Action: If you're still reading, thank you for saying *"yes"* for wanting to live your best life. Be warned—this is not a light, surface-level read. This book requires you to act and put in the work. Real change only happens when you engage with the process. But what do you have to lose? If you're unhappy now, I promise that through this journey of introspection, self-reflection, and answering challenging questions, we will uncover your true, authentic version of you and create lasting change. The change you have always wanted is to be the best version of yourself for the world to see and appreciate.

My Belief in You: You have unique value and contributions to offer the world. Through this book, I aim to help you discover your best self, gain direction, and build the confidence to share your unique gifts and purpose. Higher self-esteem and confidence will empower you to show up each day and make a more positive and impactful contribution to those around you in whatever way feels meaningful to you.

Your Guide: This book is a personal journey to understand yourself better, examine your habits, and replace negative behaviours with positive ones. Most importantly, it will help you know what you truly want from this precious life we share.

Let's Begin: We are starting a life-changing journey together.

YOUR LIFE

I want you to know that it's not your fault. You are the result of a life and a world that we live in that has a way of making us feel like we're constantly falling short, trapped in a loop of stress, anxiety, and frustration. It's easy to think that the chaos in your mind and the struggles you face each day reflect who you are or what you lack. But here's the truth: you are not defined by your struggles. You are not the mess you feel inside. And most importantly, you are not alone in feeling lost.

Life throws us challenges, many of which we're not prepared for. Society teaches us to push harder, stay busy, and never show weakness. Yet, no one tells us how to silence the noise in our heads—the insecurities, the self-doubt, the fear of not being good enough. So, we bury it, hoping it will disappear. But it never does.

What if I told you that you could regain control, navigate through the fog, and emerge stronger and that the struggle is essential to your unique journey?

This book isn't about quick fixes or surface-level solutions. It's about confronting the things you've been avoiding and coming out on the other side as a stronger, more resilient version of yourself. The process won't be easy, but it will be worth it.

Throughout this journey, we'll uncover the roots of your struggles, teach you how to face them head-on and guide you towards a balanced, fulfilling and authentic life. You'll understand that the power to change has always been within you—you just needed the tools to unlock it.

You've already taken the first step by picking up this book. Now, let's walk through this path together, shoulder to shoulder, side by side.

Approach

Throughout this book, I will help you make sense of the chaos. I'll guide you through self-discovery and personal growth that will empower you to understand your struggles and transform them into opportunities for growth.

You'll find insights explaining why you feel lost, overwhelmed, or stuck, helping you see your thinking patterns and behaviour in a new light. These insights will help you recognise the root causes of your inner struggles so you can finally stop blaming yourself for feeling the way you do. It's about understanding where your pain comes from and learning how to heal from it rather than continuing to carry its weight.

With practical recommendations, I'll show you how to start making small but powerful changes in your life. These are not complicated or unattainable suggestions but simple, actionable steps you can begin immediately. You'll learn to shift your mindset, adopt healthier habits, and create a balance that works for you. Whether it's developing a more positive relationship with yourself or learning how to navigate the pressures of everyday life, these recommendations will serve as tools to help you regain control and find clarity.

The book has five sections: **Your Mind, Your Body, Your Money, Your Soul, and Your Escape**.

Each section delves into the critical elements of personal growth, exploring how to cultivate mental resilience, achieve physical strength and well-being, build financial stability, and connect with a more profound sense of purpose. By focusing on these five pillars, the book provides a holistic approach to self-improvement, helping you become the best version of yourself in every aspect of life.

One of the most essential parts of this journey will be the reflective questions I'll ask you to consider and journal. These questions will encourage you to pause, reflect, and be honest. It's easy to stay on autopilot without looking at how or why you feel, but taking time for introspection is essential to creating natural, lasting change. The questions help you dig deeper into your thoughts and emotions, revealing truths about yourself that you may have avoided.

By working through these insights, recommendations, and reflective questions, you will realise that the power to overcome your struggles has always been within you. I'm not here to provide you with all the answers—I'm here to guide you towards discovering them for yourself. The more you engage with this process, the more you will begin to understand that feeling lost in your shit isn't permanent. You can find your way out. And I'll be here with you every step of the way.

This book is about your story

While my journey is the foundation of this book, it's not about me—it's about you. I want us to start with you, where you are amid your struggles, questions, and uncertainties. I aim to gently guide you towards answers and solutions that resonate with your life, experiences, and truth.

Research suggests that many people feel dissatisfied or unhappy with their lives. According to a 2022 global survey by Gallup, about **60% of people report feeling unhappy** with some aspect of their lives, while approximately 25% report feeling consistently unhappy or dissatisfied. The primary factors cited include financial stress, work-life balance, health issues, and a lack of purpose or fulfilment. This book will address these societal issues and see how they relate to you.

As we progress through the book, I will share what I've discovered during my several decades of self-development—insights, lessons, and breakthroughs that have helped me navigate life's challenges. These are not universal answers but pieces of wisdom that might help you find your path. You can take what resonates with you, apply it to your journey, and leave behind anything that doesn't serve you.

No two paths are the same. What worked for me might not work for you similarly, and that's OK. This book is about helping you uncover what *will* work for you, and to do that, we'll begin with the most critical person in this equation: you. I'll ask you to reflect on your life, patterns, and desires. Through self-exploration, you'll find your answers—answers that are already within you but might need a little guidance to surface.

Along the way, I'll share the moments from my journey—times of struggle, growth, and transformation. These personal stories are not here to be a template for you but to show that change is possible.

I've been where you are and spent decades learning to find my way out of it. Now, I want to offer you what I've learned, hoping it will help you navigate your journey with greater clarity and confidence.

Together, we'll explore what's holding you back, what you need to let go of, and how you can move forward in a way that feels empowering and true to who you are. Self-development isn't about quick fixes or bypassing the hard work. It's about growth, becoming more self-aware, and ultimately, living a fulfilling and meaningful life.

SECTION 01
YOUR MIND

CHAPTER 1
WHY DID YOU PICK THIS BOOK UP?

Let's address the big and beautiful elephant in the room. You've picked up a book titled *'Are You Lost in Your Shit?'* which must resonate with you in some way. It's an interesting initial reflection. Please take a moment and consider it. Can you explain it, articulate it, or is it a feeling?

This initial reflection tells me something important—a part of you feels unhappy or unfulfilled.

That life hasn't turned out the way you wanted.

Do you sometimes feel like you're stuck, low, or a bit depressed?

Are you struggling with negative thoughts or self-doubt, feeling you're not good enough?

These are challenging, reflective questions, but they are essential to consider. It's common to wonder if there is more to life or that you have untapped potential and a capacity for more significant growth. Have you ever asked yourself: What is holding me back? Why do I feel this way?

Maybe you want something better for your life but don't yet know what that looks like. Do you feel like your life has a deeper meaning or purpose you haven't discovered? Or maybe you want to feel better, to be content, or to be happy—whatever that means to you? Do you ever feel like something is missing, a void inside you that you can't quite explain?

You are not alone; in fact, this feeling is widespread; 1 in 8 people, 1 billion people, are living with feelings of low self-esteem, depression or anxiety. These issues are on the rise. For example, the World Health Organization (WHO) reported a 25% increase in depression and anxiety worldwide during the COVID-19 pandemic alone, a trend that has only increased over time.

Whatever your story, you're not alone in feeling underachieving or that life is passing you by. You don't need to have all the answers right now—in fact, it's OK if you don't have any answers. This book aims to help you find those answers step by step. We're doing this together as a team.

Have you ever asked yourself what you want from this one precious life we share? What would it take to live a life where you feel truly happy or content? Do you know, or is that something you're currently searching for?

And if you feel like everything is a mess—whether on the outside or inside—you're not alone. To the world, you might look like you're doing just fine, but on the inside, maybe you're struggling, feeling like an imposter, unsure of what to do next. Do you ever feel like you're just going through the motions, doing what you're 'supposed' to do but without any joy?

Let me reassure you: it's OK to feel lost. It's OK not to have it all figured out. You don't have to have all the answers right now. Most people don't, no matter how put together they may seem on social media or in life. Behind the fake smiles and 'perfect' lives, most people are dealing with their own battles, just like you.

I understand; I've felt low for as long as I can remember. And despite what people might have seen from the outside, I always felt like I wasn't enough.

For years, I wore a mask of confidence, but beneath it, I was struggling. If this sounds familiar, I want you to know you are not alone and broken. There is hope.

Our present world has seen a global rise in anxiety, depression, and feelings of low mood due to shifts in modern society, technology, and lifestyle. Social isolation has intensified as people spend more time online and less in face-to-face interactions, leading to widespread loneliness and a decline in the sense of community and support. The feeling of isolation is made worse by social media, which often fuels self-comparison and self-esteem issues, as people frequently compare their lives to idealised, curated portrayals online. The pressures of academic and workplace environments have also intensified as people face an "always-on" culture that blurs boundaries between work, study, and personal life, often leading to stress and burnout.

Additionally, economic uncertainty, driven by rising living costs and job instability, has added significant stress for many, exacerbating feelings of anxiety. Global challenges, including health crises like COVID-19, climate change, and political tensions, contribute to an overarching sense of unpredictability and fear for the future. Together, these factors create a challenging mental health landscape, affecting people across all demographics. Though growing awareness has encouraged more people to openly discuss their mental health struggles, this increased openness also reveals a genuine rise in those facing these issues, highlighting a need for more significant support, community connection, and well-being practices.

Over the past number of decades, I've been on a journey to find a better version of myself and move into a place where I can enjoy my life—where I can enjoy *being me*. I tried so many things, hoping they would make me feel better and give me a sense of purpose. And now, I'm finally at a place where I feel clear, confident, and hopeful for the future. I wish I could have had this clarity earlier in my life—it would have saved me so much pain and confusion. But I wrote this book—to share everything I've learned and ensure you know it's not your fault and you can do something about it. You can improve your life. You can feel better, and you do deserve to feel better.

I'm not just going to share my story; I will share the tools, strategies, and resources that helped me transform my life from learning about health, fitness, and wellness to understanding money, building wealth, and investing. I've made countless mistakes. I want to help you avoid those same pitfalls, saving you decades of time and money.

Can I ask you what it would look like for you to get your shit together, to feel whole and content, to wake up every day feeling like you're moving in the right direction? Would that feel like a true-life transformation? That's _my goal for you_.

This book is a blueprint for anyone wanting to take control of their life. But it won't happen overnight. Progress is about tiny, consistent steps, day by day, working towards a better version of you. You'll need to reflect, journal, question your habits, sit with your emotions, and understand what's driving your feelings. Your journey, like any meaningful transformation, takes time and patience.

Are you ready to start taking those steps?

I've been where you are and want you to know there is hope. You *can* conquer your inner battles and live a purposeful, contented, and happiness-filled life. I'm here for you, and together, we will change your life—one tiny step at a time.

LET'S BE MATES

I want to share that I've never written a book before and have no qualifications in self-help. I'm not a trained psychologist, fitness expert, personal trainer, money or investment expert, or self-help coach. I am none of those things. I have no formal qualifications and am completely unqualified in the professional sense to give you any advice or guidance.

I have something far more valuable: experience. I have decades of experience to offer you. Decades of being where you are, I was feeling shit and turning to 'temporary solutions' like comfort food, alcohol, or getting high to make me feel better.

50% of people globally turn to alcohol, smoking, comfort food, or drugs to cope with stress; I am expecting that you are in that group, and I certainly was. I think I was the leader.

We need to be open and honest with each other; most importantly, you must be honest with yourself.

The best place for us to start is to become mates, you and me, because as you continue this journey of change, we need to talk to each other like friends. Best friends. A best friend who has your best interests at heart.

We are going to go on a journey together. This journey is going to be introspective because we are going to look at all the reasons why you feel lost and a bit shit, what's happened during your life for you to feel this way. So, we must be honest with each other. You will learn to trust me, and you will learn to trust yourself through this journey.

/// WHY DID YOU PICK THIS BOOK UP?

What I have to offer you is decades of experience of feeling like shit and a bit low and how I have learned to live a better life, more contented life. I will gently guide you through the areas I believe will make a difference in your life over the long term.

I feel like we are going somewhere. I am excited to see where this goes.

TELL ME ABOUT YOU

My commitment in this book is to focus on you, the reader, just like a good therapist would. I will only share stories of my experiences if I believe they are relevant to our topic.

This book is going to be an active process. A lot of books which you read, you read it, and that's it. You may retain the information, or you don't.

That's _not_ how this is going to work. You will need a pen and paper or a smartphone to record notes. This is how we will express your emotions and thoughts to help you feel better.

I'd recommend getting a book or a journal, something you can write in, but I don't want you to procrastinate. Any pen, paper, or smartphone is OK to get started.

If you feel that writing is not suitable for you, you can answer these questions out loud, like you are being interviewed on a podcast about your life. You can speak your answers on your smartphone or via an app.

I will refer to this action throughout this book as 'journalling'. You can speak your journalling into your smartphone or write in a journal, whichever feels good.

Please start this first exercise

Please tell me about yourself. And please, don't think about it. Just do it.

No one will read it or hear it, not even you. I never go back and read my journal entries.

Here are some questions to help you get started.

How are you feeling?
What are you proud of in your life?
What are you grateful for?
What is your happy hour today?
What are you looking forward to?

Thank you for completing this exercise. Getting started in something new often feels daunting and uncomfortable, but it is the first step toward growth and positive change. Your willingness to take this step shows courage and commitment to your well-being. Keep moving forward—each small action builds momentum toward a better, more fulfilling life.

WHY IS JOURNALING IMPORTANT?

Journaling will be a vital part of our journey together. Research shows that regular journaling can significantly improve mood and mental well-being. Journaling our thoughts and emotions for just a few minutes a day can reduce symptoms of anxiety and depression by 30-40%. Practising gratitude through journaling has increased happiness by up to 25%, providing a simple yet powerful tool for emotional clarity and resilience.

I began journaling during one of my darkest periods, and while it wasn't easy at first—sometimes, it still isn't—it allowed me to express my darkest thoughts and gradually see hope and positivity. Over time, journaling gave me perspective, helping me observe and understand my emotions and their reasons.

When I started journalling, I used to use words like "I am feeling *lost, hopeless, useless, depressed*, and *low*." Those words appear less frequently now, and you'll likely find the same as you keep journaling. Through this practice, I discovered that my emotional state would often swing between hopeful and feeling low, and the same might be true for you. Let's explore this together.

The Power of Journaling

Research highlights that journaling provides a structured way to process emotions, gain insights, and relieve stress. Expressive journaling can "offload" negative thoughts, reduce rumination, and promote a sense of calm. A study in *Psychological Science* found that putting feelings into words decreases activity in the amygdala, the brain's emotional centre, and boosts activity in the prefrontal cortex, which supports rational thinking. This shift helps create a sense of control over your emotions.

Daily journaling lets you pinpoint what is weighing you down and separate that from the rest of your life. This practice reinforces that while you may face challenges, they do not define your entire life.

How to Get Started

Daily journaling doesn't need to be complicated. Simply journal how you feel each day. This habit will become one of the most insightful parts of your day.

Buying a specific journal can be helpful. I recommend *MindJournals*. for men, as it includes prompts to help articulate feelings, which can be particularly useful for those who struggle to express themselves. For women, *The Five-Minute Journal* by Intelligent Change or *The Self-Care Journal* by Insight Editions are popular options for improving mood and self-awareness with guided prompts and reflections.

Aligning Thoughts, Emotions and Words

I realised that I had three different "voices":

1. **Thoughts (Inner Dialogue)**: My constant stream of thoughts, mainly being negative and critical.

2. **Spoken Words**: The version of me that suppressed my feelings and told everyone I was doing OK.

3. **Written Words**: The reflective, thoughtful version that appeared when I journaled.

Over time, these different "voices" began to align, allowing me to express my emotions more honestly and confidently. Research supports this: cognitive studies indicate that inner dialogue shapes self-perception and behaviour, while verbalising thoughts helps reduce stress. Writing down these thoughts allows for deeper processing, fostering self-awareness and emotional clarity.

Your First Step

I encourage you to begin journalling daily. Start each day by answering the question, *"How are you feeling today?"* and let your thoughts flow freely onto the page. This step is simple but transformative and will begin a journey towards a more contented life.

Journal, reflect and discover the power of your inner voice.

YOUR PAST, PRESENT, AND FUTURE

Let's take a moment to reflect on your life in three steps: **your past, present, and future.**

Do this in separate sessions to give yourself time to journal thoughtfully and delve deeper into each phase of your life.

Before starting, please put down this book and walk outside for a **5-minutes**.

Why? Walking boosts blood flow to the brain, enhancing mental clarity and creativity.

Stanford University research shows that a short walk can increase creative thinking by up to 60%, helping you better organise and express your thoughts.

Your Past

Start by reflecting on your childhood. Use these questions as prompts, but don't feel restricted; journal whatever comes to mind:

- How would you describe your childhood?
- What were your parents like, and how was your relationship with them?
- How did your parents' relationship with each other affect you?
- Were there any challenging experiences that shaped you?
- What was school like for you? Did you thrive or struggle? What did you enjoy or dislike about it?

Think about the choices you made after school:

- Did you go to college or university? What did you study, and why?
- Did you choose to travel or start working? What influenced those decisions?
- How did you spend those formative years after school, and what did you learn about yourself then?
- What are some of your best memories from that period?

Take your time with this exercise. It may bring up fond or challenging memories, but these reflections offer valuable insights into your motivations, choices, and passions.

Pause here and allow yourself a few days to journal, reflect, and explore your past deeply. This introspection will help you understand your present and shape your future.

Your Present

Before beginning this section, take a 10-minute walk. Bring a podcast, music, or meditation if you'd like—or enjoy the natural sounds around you. A brief walk can uplift your mood, boost circulation, sharpen your focus, support joint health, and aid digestion.

Now, let's shift our focus to your present life. Use these prompts as a guide, but feel free to answer some of them. Please journal what comes to mind and explore your current state honestly:

- How would you describe your present life?
- What aspects of your life do you enjoy?
- What challenges or frustrations are you facing?
- How does your present align with the dreams or goals you once had?
- If you could change one thing, what would it be?

The goal is to identify what's working well and pinpoint areas that need attention. This self-reflection helps highlight where we can focus our efforts for positive change.

Remember, this journey is about self-discovery. By examining your present, we can better understand why certain aspects of your life may feel unfulfilling, isolate areas for growth, and address any habits or behaviours that hold you back.

You are not alone on this journey. You are at the beginning of real, introspective work—an essential step towards living the life you desire.

They say no one is coming to rescue you, but you are here, saving yourself. You are courageous, capable, and deserving of this journey. I'm proud of you for taking these steps.

Your future

> *"The present is just that: a gift, but you will spend the rest of your life in the future, so planning it is essential."*

Please take a 15-minute walk before starting. This simple activity boosts mood, focus, and creativity by increasing blood flow and releasing endorphins, enhancing your thinking and journaling. A daily walk can transform how you feel. Whenever you need a reset or are about to start a task, take a walk—you deserve it.

Thinking about the future may seem abstract, but you might feel anxious or lost without a plan. Studies show that setting goals and planning improves motivation, reduces stress, and increases life satisfaction. Time will pass regardless, so why not steer it intentionally? Inaction today could mean being in the same place—or worse—in 10 years. Your time is your greatest asset; use it wisely.

Reflect on these essentials: **health, relationships, housing, career, finances, and time**. These are big topics, and it's okay if you don't have all the answers now. Awareness is the first step; action can follow later.

Exercise: Visualising Your Future. Take a few moments to visualise your ideal future.

Find a quiet space, close your eyes, and breathe deeply: in for 4 seconds, hold for 4, out for 4. Repeat four times. Picture your dream life in detail: where you live, who you're with, what your days look like, what excites you. Let these visions guide your writing today.

Now, journal these dream scenarios. Let your thoughts flow freely and be as vivid as possible. This exercise will help shape your vision and create a roadmap for turning dreams into reality.

Take your time, enjoy the process, and let yourself dream. Reflect, journal, walk, meditate, and breathe.

/// WHY DID YOU PICK THIS BOOK UP?

CHAPTER 1 SUMMARY

Hopefully, you are starting to feel even better and have more direction than when you first picked up this book. You've begun working through your thoughts and emotions and journaling about your past, present, and future and made significant progress.

Journaling is essential for clarity and self-reflection. Journaling your thoughts and emotions through speech or writing improves mental clarity, reduces stress, and promotes self-awareness. I rarely go back and read my entries, which allows me to express myself freely without judgment. Journaling will help you release emotions, gain perspective, and feel better. Start journaling daily—it's one of the kindest things you can do for yourself. Through journaling, you will become your own best friend.

Daily walks are transformative. Even a short walk can boost your mood, release endorphins, and clear your mind. Walking is excellent for your physical and mental health—it supports cardiovascular function, reduces stress, aids digestion, and helps maintain a healthy weight. I recommend gradually building up your walk time to 30 minutes to 1 hour daily. Walking has significantly impacted my life; what seemed like a simple activity has improved my well-being beyond measure.

Meditation I also introduced you to the 'box' breathing exercise as a foundation for meditation. This practice can help ground you and reduce overthinking. Meditation has proven benefits: it reduces stress, enhances focus, improves emotional health, and boosts self-awareness. Use apps like Aura or Calm or explore guided meditations on YouTube or Spotify. Starting your day with 10 minutes of meditation can set the tone for a calm, focused day and help you manage stress.

Conclusion The best steps to feeling better include journaling, walking, and meditation. I start each day with meditation to set my mindset, aim for 10,000 steps, and journal. If stress arises, I rely on these tools to regain balance.

Journaling, walking, and meditation are your new superpowers for feeling better and gaining self-control. They're free (or low-cost with apps) and always available to support you. Make these practices your secret strengths. The more you use them, the stronger you'll become mentally and physically.

You're more resilient than you realise.

I believe in you. You can do this.

> Before starting Chapter 2, please incorporate journaling, walking, and meditating into your daily routine. These three daily practices are the foundations of our growth.

CHAPTER 2
INTRODUCTION TO MASLOW'S HIERARCHY OF HUMAN NEEDS

We've covered a lot so far and gotten to know each other. You've started journaling, walking, and meditating—and found your new secret superpowers. These practices are helping you become more in tune with your moods, energy, and life experiences.

My goal throughout this book is to give you practical, actionable insights. The more awareness and knowledge you gain, the better you can navigate your emotions, thoughts, and behaviours. I am interested in psychology and believe there are universal frameworks that can guide everyone through life's journey and challenges.

One of these foundational frameworks is Maslow's Hierarchy of Needs, created by Abraham Maslow in 1943. This model explains human motivation through a pyramid of needs divided into five levels. It suggests that one must achieve physiological and safety needs before one can progress to fulfilling psychological needs such as love, esteem, and ultimately, self-actualisation—the pursuit of becoming one's best self and realising one's potential.

Understanding this framework is essential, especially if you feel stuck, overwhelmed, or unsure of your path. It can provide reassurance and a roadmap for improving your life step by step. You might even realise that

/// INTRODUCTION TO MASLOW'S HIERARCHY OF HUMAN NEEDS

you're already doing better than you thought when you see how your life aligns with Maslow's pyramid.

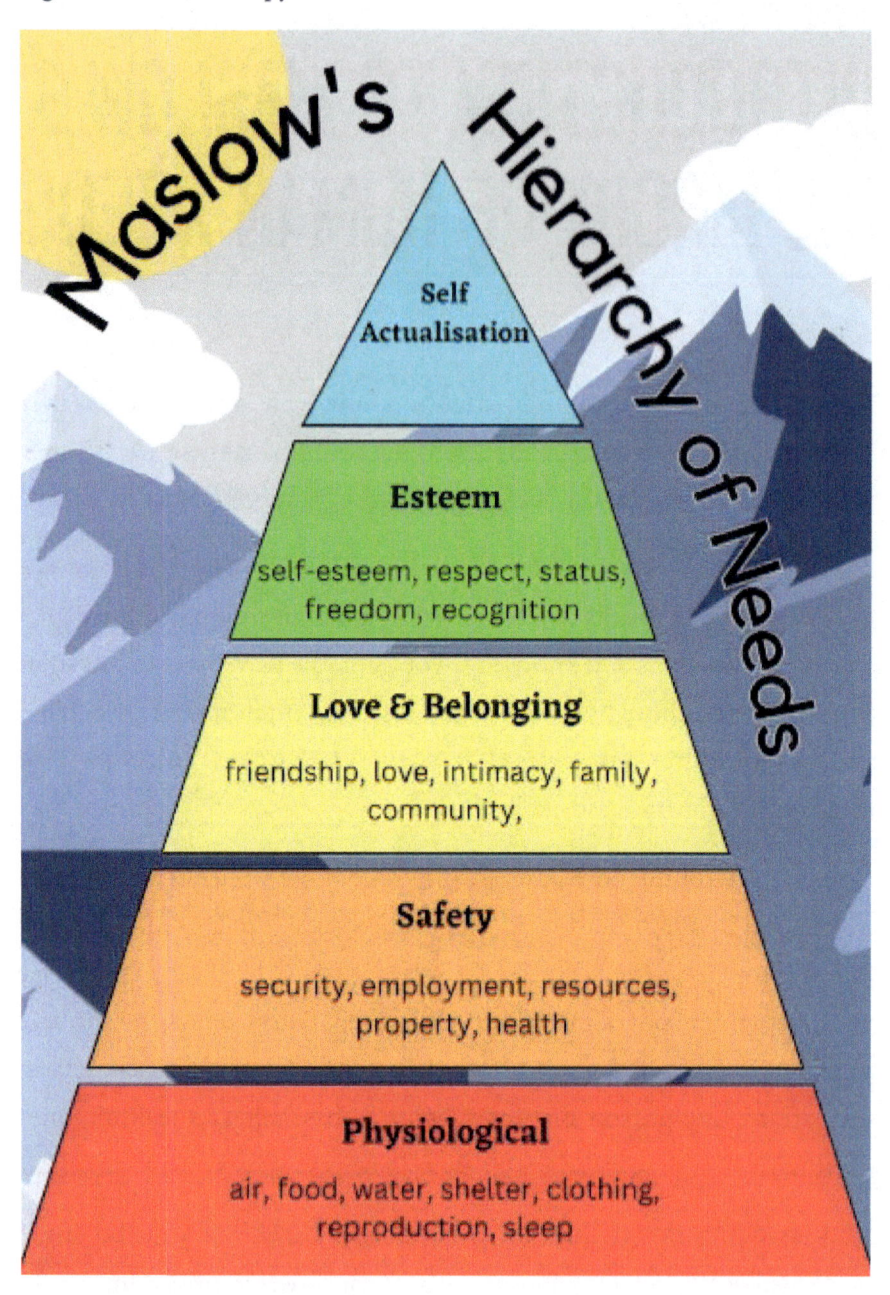

Maslow's Hierarchy of Needs

Self Actualisation

Esteem
self-esteem, respect, status, freedom, recognition

Love & Belonging
friendship, love, intimacy, family, community,

Safety
security, employment, resources, property, health

Physiological
air, food, water, shelter, clothing, reproduction, sleep

Look at the pyramid and reflect: What needs have you already met, and where do you want to see improvements?

I encourage you to journal about this and explore how your current life fits within Maslow's framework.

Maslow explained

Maslow's hierarchy shows a pyramid divided into five levels:

1. **Physiological Needs (Base of the Pyramid)**: The most basic human requirements for survival are food, water, air, shelter, sleep, and clothing.
2. **Safety Needs**: While basic needs are our foundation, the focus shifts to security and protection from physical and emotional harm, which includes personal and financial security, health, accident safety, and stable employment.
3. **Love and Belonging Needs**: After achieving safety, the need for social connections becomes essential. This level is about forming meaningful relationships and a sense of community, including friendship, intimacy, family, and social connections, such as clubs, workgroups, or religious communities.
4. **Esteem Needs**: This stage includes the need for self-esteem and recognition from others. It's about being valued and respected, which includes confidence, achievement, recognition, status, and reputation.
5. **Self-actualisation (Top of the Pyramid)** is the pinnacle of Maslow's hierarchy. It is focused on reaching one's full potential and personal growth, which includes pursuing meaningful goals, creative expression, lifelong learning, and achieving peak experiences.

Understanding these levels can help you assess your current situation and where you might need to focus for growth and fulfilment.

Maslow and your life

A professional athlete is a prime example of self-actualisation. Throughout their career, they fully embody their passion and meet all levels of Maslow's hierarchy. They belong to structured communities such as teams or clubs, earn a living, continuously develop their skills, and strive for excellence.

This daily pursuit enables them to align with their purpose and reach the peak of personal fulfilment.

For most of us, reaching self-actualisation is more complex, with varied needs, goals, and shifting aspirations. A helpful exercise is a 'gap analysis': assess where you currently stand and where you want to be. The gap between these points forms your action plan. Revisit your vision from the previous chapter and shape it into a tangible, attainable future. Use Maslow's hierarchy as a guide, focusing on growth that leads to self-esteem (level 4) and, ultimately, self-actualisation (level 5).

Reflect on these questions to guide your journey:

- What would make you genuinely proud when you look back at your life at 80?
- What would you regret not doing when looking back?
- What is missing in your life today?

Please be patient and kind to yourself. If you feel lost or unsure, know that the answers are already within you, just waiting to be discovered. Your life, your choices—this is the luxury of being human.

Take a moment to close your eyes and breathe. Envision a future where you have fully realised your potential. Where are you? What are you doing? Who is with you?

Change takes effort, and life can be challenging, but with clarity and intention, it's possible. Please journal, reflect, and take your time. This process is transformative.

You're doing great, and I'm proud of your progress. Keep going.

CHAPTER 3
THE BIG PROBLEM

Here's the fundamental issue with everything I've just outlined:

You may achieve your dream, reach self-actualisation, and still feel miserable, anxious, or even more depressed. You could be successful, financially secure, and surrounded by respect but still feel inadequate. You feel like you are not enough. By why?

Success does not guarantee happiness or fill the void inside of you.

Maslow and the Problem

Maslow's Hierarchy of Needs was groundbreaking in 1943 and serves as a solid framework for understanding human motivation. Throughout my life, I pursued this model: I secured a good job, a house, a loving family, a supportive community, and professional respect. I reached the top of this mountain, yet I didn't feel fulfilled. Realising that I had spent years striving to end up feeling worse made the situation even more confusing and painful.

The dream sold by Maslow seemed natural but ultimately felt like an illusion—a vision that didn't account for the whole picture.

Did Maslow help guide my path? Absolutely. It provided a roadmap and some answers. But why did achieving everything on that map leave me feeling emptier than before? Ironically, I was happier during the climb—when I had a purpose, drive, and hope for what reaching the top might bring. But now, standing at the top of the mountain, I felt exposed, unprepared, and suddenly aware of all the other mountains that I chose not to climb. Worse still, I realised I was on the wrong mountain entirely. Decades of work, and for what? I didn't achieve happiness; it was a self-made trap.

The realisation hit hard: I had succeeded in the external world but ignored the internal one. That's the flaw in Maslow's model—it addresses our outward journey but neglects the inward one.

Even after "achieving" success, we can still experience pain, unresolved issues, destructive habits, and self-sabotage. The real work lies deeper. We have yet to begin to explore the real, underlying struggles.

Reading about Maslow and reflecting might leave you frustrated. Imagine spending decades climbing a mountain to discover you were chasing the wrong goal (e.g. money). This was my life journey.

This book aims to prevent you from wasting your precious time and save you from years of misplaced effort, disappointment and feelings of depression.

THE ABYSS

Let's take a different approach. We've spent some time getting to know each other, and I'm beginning to understand how you feel.

I wonder if you feel something like this?

You're alone, staring into a vast, dark abyss—the overwhelming emptiness, confusion, and fear. Your mind races with relentless thoughts, and feelings of sadness, anxiety, or hopelessness take over. You're simply getting through each day, just surviving.

/// THE BIG PROBLEM

This book aims to guide you towards feeling like this:

It is a similar scene but with a crucial difference—light ahead. That light represents hope, clarity, and a sense of direction. It shows you the path forward, allowing you to move confidently into the future. It signifies a calm, kind, and steady mind. You may even find yourself enjoying the journey. That's the vision: helping you find the way out of your inner struggles and become a better you.

WHAT IS THE ABYSS?

The Abyss represents the external factors affecting how you feel. To start improving, we need to identify these influences, including substances or vices in your life.

Reflect honestly: Have you consumed any of these lately?

- **Alcohol**: Initially relaxing but often leading to anxiety and mood swings.
- **Nicotine**: Temporarily calming but highly addictive.
- **Sugar**: Quick energy followed by mood crashes.
- **Processed Foods**: Low nutrition, contributing to lethargy and low mood.
- **Stimulants, Drugs, Sleeping Pills, Diet Pills**: Immediate effects with long-term consequences.

These substances, often seen as harmless comforts, can become emotional crutches. I've been there, using alcohol and other substances as relief from stress and restlessness. They were a quick escape but never addressed the underlying feelings. Like many, I celebrated or commiserated life with these indulgences that only reinforced negative cycles.

Now, think about your life. What do you consume for comfort? Is it chocolate, binge-eating, or drinks with friends? What role do these substances play in your life? These quick fixes may feel like rewards, but they might keep you stuck.

Ask yourself: When you envisioned your future, did these habits appear in your dreams or goals? Likely not. They're not part of the vision of success or happiness. So, when will you start addressing them? Pursuing external achievements without internal peace will lead to feeling more lost, stressed, and unfulfilled.

How will you soothe yourself when you reach your goals and responsibilities increase? It's time to confront what holds you back and build healthier coping mechanisms for a future without temporary comforts.

THE ROLE OF DOPAMINE AND YOUR HABITS

Dopamine, a key neurotransmitter, regulates mood, motivation, reward, and pleasure. It drives satisfaction when we engage in activities like eating, socialising, or achieving goals. While balanced dopamine levels support motivation and focus, imbalances can lead to depression and anxiety. In essence, dopamine fuels the "feel-good" sensation of reward.

The Downside of Fast Dopamine

Quick dopamine hits from instant gratification can create harmful cycles:

- **Overstimulation**: Rapid spikes condition the brain to seek repeated rewards.
- **Desensitisation**: Repeated hits reduce dopamine receptor responsiveness, requiring more for the same pleasure.
- **Dependence**: Cravings for quick rewards overshadow meaningful, long-term goals.
- **Reduced Motivation**: Slow-reward activities seem less appealing, leading to procrastination.
- **Emotional Impact**: Reliance on instant hits often results in dissatisfaction and mood instability.

Activities providing quick dopamine bursts—like social media, junk food, shopping, and substance use—offer short-term pleasure but erode long-term well-being.

Realising True Well-being

Success or material gains don't always equate to happiness. Long-term fulfilment comes from inner growth and self-awareness, not external achievements. Research supports that true happiness is achieved and sustained through the following:

- **Hedonic Adaptation**: Temporary boosts from achievements fade; lasting contentment requires self-acceptance and gratitude.
- **Self-Determination**: Autonomy, growth, and compassion are essential for more profound satisfaction.
- **Inner Resilience**: Practices like mindfulness and journaling enhance emotional well-being.
- **Balanced Wealth**: Beyond essential financial stability, personal growth and relationships are more impactful for long-term happiness.

Take time to reflect and write honestly:

- What substances or habits dominate your life?
- What cycles keep you stuck?
- How much sugar, alcohol, or processed food have you consumed recently?
- What role does health play for your future self?

Consider this: If you stay the same, who will you become in 10 years? Take a moment and journal. Awareness is the first step to transformation.

THE MIND

Let's redefine addiction—it might surprise you.

Addiction is when a person cannot stop using a substance or engaging in a behaviour despite harmful consequences. These actions trigger the brain's reward system, releasing dopamine and creating pleasure or relief. Over time, the brain craves these feelings, leading to repeated use and increased tolerance. The person needs more substance or activity to feel the same level of pleasure, even as health, relationships, or finances suffer.

Addiction isn't limited to drugs or alcohol; it includes behaviours like excessive gaming, social media use, or even consuming refined sugar. Sugar acts like a drug in the body, driving cravings and reinforcing the cycle. What starts as a moment of comfort or reward becomes the source of the problem.

To be clear, eating sugary or processed foods isn't the same as using hard drugs. I'm not a therapist, so if you're struggling with severe addiction, seeking professional help is essential. However, understanding that these substances impact your well-being and happiness is crucial.

Think about this: If you eat one piece of chocolate, do you crave another? If we share a glass of wine, do you reach for a second glass? Fast food often leaves you unsatisfied, prompting more cravings. It's no accident—foods and drinks are engineered for irresistible appeal, activating dopamine and reinforcing consumption.

Now, consider natural foods: Do you devour plain grilled chicken or fresh fruit uncontrollably? Likely not. Profit-driven companies design processed, high-sugar foods to keep you hooked, sacrificing your health for their bottom line. It's no wonder 74% of Americans are overweight or obese—this surge coincides with the rise of processed, nutrient-poor foods over the last 50 years. Most supermarket items are artificial substances, not natural food.

The very things you turn to for comfort can trap you. This reliance becomes an emotional crutch, akin to Stockholm syndrome: you cling to what harms you.

When you crave chocolate or need a drink, you miss the chance to experience true peace, clarity, and joy. I know this because I've been free from these traps for several years. My body is regulated, my mind is clear, and I've shed weight without effort or strict dieting. Life now feels full of potential, hope, and excitement. That's why I wrote this book—your best self awaits on the other side of what you consume.

If you think, "A little indulgence isn't so bad," remember that picking up this book shows that excess might impact you more than you admit. Awareness is step one. The real question is why we turn to these substances for emotional support and how we can reduce this reliance.

The core issue isn't just the substance but often unresolved trauma or stress. It's time to understand that your self-prescribed comforts, over time, may have serious consequences.

Next, I'll share stories of people who achieved great success but tragically lost their lives due to substance reliance.

Disclaimer:

This content discusses topics related to death and alcohol abuse, which some readers may find sensitive or triggering. If you or someone you know is struggling, please seek support from qualified professionals or organisations specialising in these issues.

THE WONDERFUL AMY WINEHOUSE

Many know the brilliant yet tragic story of Amy Winehouse. The British singer-songwriter, celebrated for her distinctive voice and soulful blend of jazz, soul, and rhythm and blues, achieved fame with her hit album *Back to Black*, earning five Grammy Awards. Her music, marked by raw and honest lyrics, mirrored her battles with addiction and mental health. Despite her success, Amy's struggles became public, culminating in her untimely death from alcohol poisoning at just 27.

Amy's story, like many others, illustrates that even reaching the pinnacle of success—self-actualisation—does not safeguard against deeper issues. Celebrities like Jimi Hendrix, Janis Joplin, Whitney Houston, and more recently, individuals like Liam Payne, showcase a pattern: success and fame can come with immense pressure that, if not handled with care and support, may lead to substance abuse or tragic outcomes.

While it's easy to focus on high-profile cases, the reality is that everyday people face similar struggles—without the resources, visibility, or support systems available to celebrities. For many, life feels like a battle, marked by financial stress, loneliness, and an overwhelming sense of survival. The struggle is real for those trying to balance work, relationships, and personal well-being, often in isolation. The fight against self-sabotage, unhealthy coping mechanisms, and daily life pressures can be relentless.

Highlighting these stories doesn't deter you from success but reminds you that accurate fulfilment and resilience come from understanding and addressing internal battles. Without this groundwork, the very achievements you strive for could amplify your struggles. The key to achieving your goals

/// THE BIG PROBLEM

is to be emotionally well-equipped to sustain your achievements and be in a state of well-being.

Actual growth involves "doing the work" now—so when you succeed, you can navigate the challenges that come with it without falling apart.

LET'S RETURN TO YOUR CHILDHOOD AND FIND THE ROOT CAUSES OF YOUR EMOTIONAL DISCOMFORT

As I've mentioned, I'm not a therapist or psychologist. My aim here is to foster awareness. If you wish to explore these topics further, seeking professional guidance is highly recommended to understand better your childhood and any underlying traumas affecting you.

Research strongly supports the connection between childhood experiences and emotional well-being later in life. Here's a summary of key findings:

Attachment Theory and Relationship Patterns: Research by John Bowlby and expanded by Mary Ainsworth shows that early attachment styles—secure, anxious, avoidant, or disorganised—shape how we relate to others as adults. Understanding these patterns helps form healthier relationships and manage emotional responses.

Adverse Childhood Experiences (ACEs): Studies by the CDC and Kaiser Permanente highlight a strong link between childhood trauma and increased risks of depression, anxiety, and other emotional issues in adulthood. Recognising and working through these experiences with support can improve resilience and mental health.

Inner Child Work and Trauma Processing: Approaches such as inner child work and cognitive behavioural therapy (CBT) focus on revisiting childhood experiences to reframe and heal unresolved emotional wounds. Research published in *The Journal of Trauma & Dissociation* shows that addressing these unmet childhood needs can significantly reduce symptoms of depression, anxiety, and PTSD, aiding in better emotional regulation.

Self-Compassion and Emotional Resilience: Psychologist Kristin Neff's studies indicate that understanding one's childhood fosters self-compassion. This awareness allows individuals to be more forgiving toward themselves, enhancing resilience and reducing self-criticism.

In summary, delving into childhood experiences can provide insight into current emotional challenges, helping to reframe limiting beliefs, build healthier coping strategies, and support long-term emotional well-being.

PROFESSIONAL SUPPORT

Therapy and journaling are powerful tools for exploring childhood and past experiences, offering profound insights that can lead to emotional healing. Therapy provides a safe space to unpack your personal history, guided by a professional who helps you identify and process memories that may still influence your present behaviour and emotions. This structured exploration can reveal hidden beliefs or coping mechanisms formed in response to childhood events, clarifying how these patterns manifest in your adult life.

Journaling complements therapy by allowing for ongoing self-reflection and introspection outside of sessions. Journaling thoughts, emotions, and memories helps crystallise experiences, making understanding and processing them easier. By revisiting these reflections, you gain an awareness that deepens your therapy experience, helping to bridge the gap between sessions and foster continuous self-awareness and growth.

Both therapy and journaling encourage confronting and validating complicated feelings. Acknowledging the emotions you've pushed aside helps you recognise how certain past events shaped your self-perception and reactions. This validation is crucial for breaking negative cycles and reframing your relationship with those experiences, empowering you to move forward with greater self-compassion.

Therapy helps dissect and reframe how childhood experiences contribute to current thoughts and habits. For instance, if you developed perfectionism or people-pleasing tendencies from seeking validation as a child, therapy can help you understand why these behaviours started and guide you in shifting to healthier patterns. Journaling supports this by providing a non-judgmental space where you can document moments when these tendencies surface, helping you identify triggers and monitor your progress.

Exploring your past through therapy and journaling can also highlight unresolved trauma or lingering insecurities that fuel self-doubt or low self-esteem. This awareness helps you better understand your emotional responses, enabling you to develop healthier coping mechanisms. By Journaling, you create a narrative that integrates these memories, allowing you to process them from a more grounded perspective.

Engaging in both practices builds emotional resilience and strengthens one's sense of self. When you understand and process your story, you can begin to connect the dots and understand yourself better, recognising that your reactions today often have roots in yesterday's experiences. This self-awareness lays the foundation for transformative change, fostering acceptance and reducing self-criticism.

Ultimately, therapy and journaling together provide a powerful pathway to healing. By revisiting and reinterpreting your past, you reshape how you see yourself in the present and empower yourself to approach the future more clearly and confidently. This combined approach helps dismantle limiting beliefs and paves the way for a more authentic and fulfilled life.

Reflecting on your childhood can be eye-opening and transformative. Consider these questions:

- What moments from your childhood stand out the most?
- Are there any unresolved issues or patterns you still carry into adulthood?
- What are these behaviours or patterns, and how do they appear in your life?
- What is the negative consequence of these behaviours?
- When you connect the dots, what cycles are you caught in?

Journaling your responses can be an impactful first step toward uncovering and understanding these experiences. While this self-exploration can be powerful, working with a professional can guide you further, as some insights might be buried deep in your subconscious. This work is challenging but invaluable—it clarifies your present behaviours and reactions.

This journey is one of self-discovery and personal growth. It's about healing past wounds, understanding yourself better, and reclaiming your life. Through this process, you can cultivate self-acceptance, find hope, and break free from negative patterns. Remember, you are enough—and soon, you will believe it too.

YOUR INNER CHILD

Understanding Your Inner Child and Its Impact

The *inner child* refers to the part of your subconscious that holds childhood memories, emotions, and experiences. It embodies both the positive traits of childhood—joy, curiosity, and innocence—and unresolved emotional wounds that can affect adult behaviour. These unhealed aspects may manifest as low self-esteem, emotional reactivity, or relationship difficulties.

The Importance of Inner Child Work

Inner child work is a therapeutic approach that reconnects you with your younger self, acknowledging and healing unmet emotional needs. This active process promotes growth, emotional well-being, and self-love. It involves practices like meditation, writing letters to your inner child, and reparenting yourself with compassion.

Examples of Inner Child Work

- **Inner Child Meditation**: Visualise comforting your younger self, offering reassurance and love.
- **Writing Letters**: Acknowledge your inner child's pain and unmet needs with kindness.
- **Dialogue**: Have conversations with your inner child, listening and responding empathetically.
- **Reparenting**: Become your supportive figure by setting boundaries and validating your emotions.
- **Creative Play**: Engage in fun activities to reconnect with joy and spontaneity.

Signs You May Need Inner Child Work

- Difficulty managing emotions or frequent outbursts.
- Low self-worth or a fear of abandonment.
- Self-sabotage or perfectionism.
- Struggling to maintain healthy relationships.

The Role of Professional Support

While self-reflection and journaling are powerful, working with a therapist is crucial for more profound healing. Therapists can guide you through inner child work, helping you make sense of past experiences and their impact on current behaviour. Therapy can provide relief and insight that is difficult to achieve alone.

Where to Seek Help

- **Online Therapy**: Platforms like BetterHelp and Talkspace.
- **Private Clinics**: Professional one-on-one sessions.
- **Charities and Support Groups**: Organisations like Mind and Samaritans.
- **Employee Assistance Programmes**: Offered by many workplaces.
- **University Counselling Services**: Free support for students.

Addressing your inner child fosters self-acceptance, emotional resilience, and healthier relationships with others and yourself. This work leads to long-lasting change and a more fulfilling life.

> *"Wherever you go, there you are."* – *Jon Kabat-Zinn*

Embrace this journey. Healing begins with awareness and self-compassion. I am proud of you for taking this important step.

RAPID TRANSFORMATIONAL THERAPY (RTT)

Rapid Transformational Therapy (RTT), developed by British therapist Marisa Peer, is a groundbreaking approach that blends hypnotherapy, psychotherapy, neuro-linguistic programming (NLP), and cognitive behavioural therapy (CBT). RTT aims to deliver fast and effective results by accessing the subconscious mind to identify and resolve deep-rooted emotional and psychological issues.

Why RTT Stands Out

- **Hypnosis for Deep Access**: RTT uses hypnosis to reach a relaxed state, unlocking the subconscious where core beliefs and behaviours reside.
- **Finding Root Causes**: It goes beyond treating symptoms to uncover the origin of emotional struggles, making change more profound and lasting.
- **Reprogramming the Mind**: RTT facilitates lasting change by addressing limiting beliefs and replacing them with empowering ones.
- **Fast Results**: Most people experience significant improvement in just one session, unlike traditional therapy, which may take months or years.
- **Personalised Approach**: Each session is tailored to the individual's needs, ensuring focused and effective healing.

How RTT Helps RTT is known for effectively treating issues like phobias, addictions, low self-esteem, trauma, and harmful habits. For instance, people who struggle with emotional eating may find it hard to break the cycle because it's rooted in childhood trauma, where somebody might have eaten for comfort. RTT accesses the subconscious to reveal and reframe these early experiences, allowing individuals to release old patterns and develop a healthier relationship with food and other challenges.

Steps to Access RTT

1. **Find a Certified Therapist**: Use the official RTT website (rtt.com) or other reputable directories to locate qualified practitioners.
2. **Consider Online Sessions**: Many RTT therapists offer remote therapy, providing flexibility if in-person sessions aren't available locally.
3. **Contact and Inquire**: Contact therapists to discuss session details, pricing, and formats.
4. **Book a Free Consultation**: Many therapists offer initial consultations to assess fit and address questions before scheduling a session.

A Personal Note

Engaging in RTT was transformative during my most challenging period. One session brought more relief than months of traditional therapy. Listening to the follow-up hypnotherapy recordings reinforced my progress. The therapist's supportive and kind approach made it a reflective and rewarding experience.

If you are struggling with emotional issues, I recommend that you research RTT. Lean in, trust the process, and embrace the opportunity to create lasting change and freedom.

Find out how RTT can help you at www.rtt.com

/// THE BIG PROBLEM

CHAPTER 3 SUMMARY

At the end of Chapter 2, you may have felt hopeful after learning about Maslow's 1943 roadmap to self-actualisation, guiding you through life's stages to reach your highest potential. While Maslow's hierarchy is a valuable framework, achieving self-actualisation does not guarantee happiness.

Reaching the top of your career might come with relentless stress and pressure. Being a doctor may fulfil your purpose to help others, but it also exposes you to trauma, resource limitations, and emotional exhaustion. A vet's life-saving work comes with the heartbreak of loss. The reality is that any job or life pursuit can bring significant stress.

Stress is unavoidable, a fact as certain as death and taxes. Maslow's model, created in 1943, couldn't predict the modern world's relentless pressure. As you strive for career and financial success, you must prioritise self-care to navigate stress and enjoy life's journey.

Daily habits like meditation, walking, and journaling are accessible, free, and powerful ways to reduce stress and boost joy without negatively impacting health.

I'll share a shocking statistic. The World Health Organization estimates that 80% of modern deaths are preventable with better lifestyle choices and habits. That's 80% of people losing their precious lives due to unmanaged daily habits like smoking, drinking alcohol, eating sugar and highly processed foods.

Working with a therapist can be transformative, especially when exploring options like Rapid Transformational Therapy (RTT). If you've been struggling with an issue your whole life, RTT can help you break free.

Take this chapter as an invitation to prioritise self-care, reflect deeply, and be patient with yourself. You're embarking on an essential journey of transformation and growth.

CHAPTER 3
YOUR HABIT CYCLES

Positive Habits

One of the most impactful books I recommend is *Atomic Habits* by James Clear. It teaches that small, daily habits, compounded over time, lead to remarkable results. If you want a different future, it begins with tiny behavioural changes today.

The Power of Small Steps

Instead of setting an ambitious goal like going to the gym regularly (where research shows 60-80% stop after a few months), start with tiny steps. Here's how the *Atomic Habits* approach might look:

Example: Building a Walking Routine

- **Day 1**: Choose a consistent time (e.g., 8 am daily).
- **Day 2**: At 8 am, put on your trainers and stand outside.
- **Day 3**: Walk for 1 minute.
- **Day 4**: Walk for 2 minutes.
- **Day 5**: Walk for 4 minutes.
- **Day 6**: Walk for 6 minutes.
- **Day 7**: Walk for 10 minutes.

By day 30, you could walk for 30 minutes daily without being overwhelmed, gradually building yourself up. The habit would become natural, part of your daily routine, and build confidence.

The vital part is that it starts with a ridiculously easy first few steps, e.g., Choosing a time, standing outside, and walking for one minute.

Example: Adding Strength Training

- **Day 1**: 1 rep of a bodyweight exercise (e.g., press-up or squat).
- **Day 2**: 2 reps.
- **Day 3**: 4 reps.
- **Day 4**: 8 reps.
- **Day 5**: 12 reps.
- **Day 6**: 15 reps.
- **Day 7**: 20 reps.

Within a month, you could perform over 100 reps or a combination of exercises—a goal that may now seem out of reach.

Reflection Time

In Chapter 1, I suggested starting daily walks.

- Did you start?
- Are you consistent?
- Are you holding yourself accountable for positive change?

Think of how you'll feel after 30 days of committing to this. Proud, energised, and full of evidence that you can create lasting change. The key is starting with a straightforward step today.

Set Your Time

What time will you go for a walk tomorrow? Start this simple habit loop and watch it transform over the next 30 days.

Act now and build habits that empower your future.

NEGATIVE HABITS

Conversely, we should consider how negative habits build over time.

I want to introduce you to a process flow demonstrating negative habit cycles, which often originate from unresolved childhood trauma.

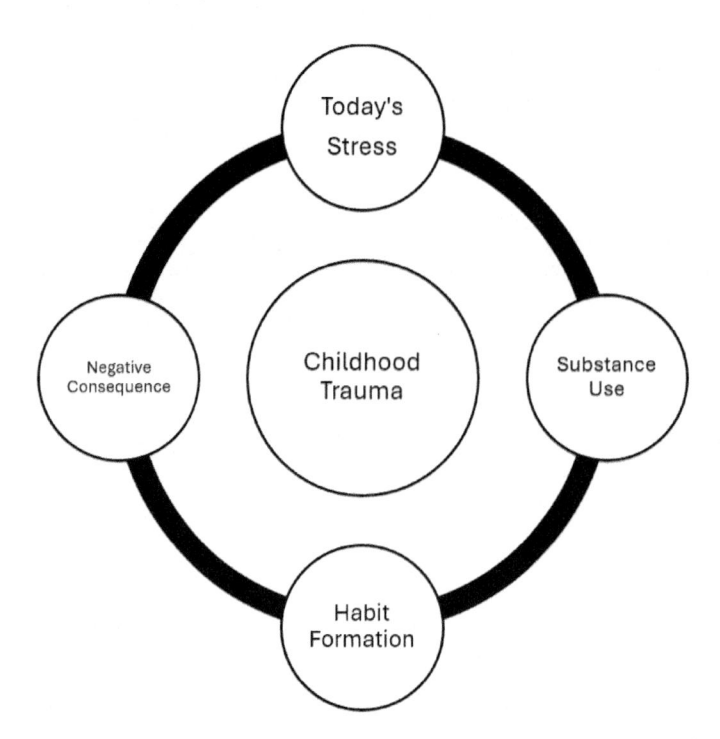

1. **Childhood Trauma**: The starting point and a root cause that can create underlying emotional distress. Trauma from childhood may resurface later in life as unresolved issues.
2. **Today's Stress**: Current stressors in life (e.g., work, relationships, financial pressures) trigger emotional discomfort. These triggers often resonate with unresolved childhood trauma, intensifying their impact.

3. **Substance Use**: In response to stress, an individual might turn to substances (e.g., alcohol, drugs, or comfort foods) as a coping mechanism to temporarily numb or alleviate their emotional discomfort. Doing so provides a short-lived relief but does not address the underlying issues.
4. **Negative Consequence**: Substance use leads to adverse outcomes such as health problems, strained relationships, or emotional guilt. These consequences create additional stress and feed back into the cycle.
5. **Habit Formation**: Repeated use of substances in response to stress solidifies the behaviour into a habit. This habit then becomes an automatic stress response, reinforcing the cycle.

In essence, the diagram represents how stress, unresolved trauma, and negative coping strategies can create a self-reinforcing cycle that is difficult to break without intervention or self-awareness.

Let's take a practical look at modern-day life.

What's Creating Stress?

An intelligent approach might be to identify and address stress at its source. Here are everyday modern stressors:

- **Work pressures**: Long hours, high demands, job insecurity, poor work-life balance.
- **Financial worries**: Rising costs, debt, and future uncertainties.
- **Technology overload**: Constant connectivity leading to mental fatigue.
- **Health issues**: Chronic illness, lack of sleep, and unhealthy habits.
- **Relationship struggles**: Family or friendship conflicts, breakups.
- **Societal expectations**: Norms, social comparisons, and pressure to conform.

- **Environment**: Urban noise, overcrowding, limited green spaces.
- **Time management**: Overcommitment, feeling there's never enough time.

As you can see, modern stress can come from every part of life. As our lives get busier, we become more successful and have families, making life more stressful. There is no escaping it; it's a fact of life.

The key is to accept that stress is a part of everyday life and focus on managing your response.

FINDING A BETTER WAY TO RESPOND

Let's look at your routine.

When you get home from work, do you feel stressed? What is your typical response? How often do you reach for your substance of choice to help soothe yourself from the day?

Research indicates that individuals employ a variety of positive and negative responses to stress, with significant implications for their mental and physical health.

Negative Responses to Stress

A 2018 survey by the Mental Health Foundation in the UK revealed that:

- **46%** of respondents reported overeating or consuming unhealthy foods due to stress.
- **29%** increased their alcohol intake when stressed.
- **16%** turned to smoking or smoked more under stress.

These behaviours can lead to adverse health outcomes, including weight gain, substance dependence, and increased risk of chronic diseases.

Positive Responses to Stress

Conversely, engaging in healthy coping mechanisms can mitigate stress's adverse effects. For example, regular physical activity, such as walking, has been shown to reduce stress levels and improve mood. A study published in *Current Psychology* found that nature-based walking interventions significantly decreased stress and anxiety among participants.

Impact of Stress Perception

An individual's perception of stress also plays a crucial role in their response. Viewing stress as a challenge rather than a threat can lead to more adaptive coping strategies. A review in the *Annals of Behavioural Medicine* highlighted that positive stress beliefs are associated with healthier behavioural responses and better health outcomes.

These findings underscore the importance of promoting positive stress responses and perceptions to enhance overall well-being.

Pause and Reflect

When stress hits, what will your response be? You are not hungry, but you walk to the kitchen, and what do you reach for?

Would it be possible not to go to the kitchen? Instead, can you walk outside? This would help with your daily step count and burn calories, contributing to your overall health goal.

There is power in the moment before you respond. You are in control.

In that moment of decision, ask yourself:

- What is happening inside me?
- Why do I feel triggered?
- What specifically caused my stress?
- Is my response reasonable?
- Can I challenge this feeling?
- Can I ignore the feeling or distract myself?

That moment before you act is decisive. You can use it to choose a better response; walk and distract yourself, and the craving will pass. Instead, feel proud of yourself. In these small, seemingly insignificant moments, you can make lasting changes.

My example

When I feel triggered or stressed, whether through frustration or any unsettling emotion, I no longer reach for a quick fix. Instead, I walk. The stronger the emotion, the longer the walk. I remind myself that the feeling will pass; an early night's sleep is my safety net if it lingers. Waking up refreshed the next day, without regret or the aftereffects of emotional eating or drinking Alcohol, is empowering. Starting your day feeling healthy and proud is achievable, transformative and addictive in a good way. You are rewarded by feeling great when you wake up. You had a good day, you did well, and you have built evidence that you are transforming, one moment and one day at a time, and you can make this change to improve your life.

Movement helps dissipate negative emotions while contributing to my health routine and motivating me to hit my daily step count. Over the years, my emotional response to eating or drinking alcohol has become non-existent. Through neuroplasticity—our brain's ability to rewire itself—my mind craves walking. When I feel stressed, I walk. My positive behaviour becomes reinforced, and choosing a healthier path becomes second nature.

Healthy Responses to Stress

Your approach to stress management can be unique to you. While walking works wonders for me and forms part of my proactive self-care routine, there are plenty of other ways to reduce stress and regain balance. Here are some options to consider proactively decreasing stress.

Physical Activities

- Yoga, running, swimming, cycling, dancing, strength training, pilates, stretching, gardening, tai chi, hiking, rock climbing, team sports, and martial arts.

Mindfulness and Relaxation Practices

- Options include meditation, deep breathing exercises, progressive muscle relaxation, visualisation, gratitude journaling, sound therapy, aromatherapy, mindful colouring or drawing.

Social and Emotional Activities

- Spending time with loved ones, talking to a therapist, engaging in hobbies, joining community groups, volunteering, pet therapy, laughing, journaling, acts of kindness, and creative activities.

Rest and Recovery

- Short naps, prioritising good sleep, spa treatments or massages, hot baths or saunas, disconnecting from technology.

Cognitive and Reflective Activities

- Learning new skills, reading, puzzles, mindful eating, positive affirmations, goal setting, and moments of silence.

Connection with Nature

- Forest bathing, beach walks, stargazing, camping, birdwatching.

Nutritional and Hydration Practices

- Eating whole foods, staying hydrated, herbal teas, limiting caffeine and sugar.

Creativity and Expression

- Playing an instrument, writing, photography, sculpting or pottery.

Spiritual Practices

- Prayer, reading spiritual texts, attending gatherings.

Lifestyle Changes

- Setting boundaries, effective time management, decluttering, minimalism.

Find what works best for you and embrace it. Every small choice adds up to a bigger transformation. Choose to respond in a way that builds the best version of yourself.

Get your trainers. Step outside. Walk, think, and reflect on who you are becoming.

The best version of you is waiting.

ARE YOU SURVIVING OR THRIVING?

Are you surviving each day or genuinely thriving? Are your days filled with stress, only to seek relief in the evenings? Or do you come home refreshed, ready for the next day? If you're reading this, you're likely in survival mode—but there's a better way.

For years, I searched for answers. The truth? It was always simple: eat well, meditate, journal, walk, exercise, and follow a self-care routine. These habits are the keys to thriving. Yet, many stay stuck in survival mode, gripped by the fight-or-flight response. This primal reaction, meant for real danger, is now triggered by daily stress—work, social conflicts, and finances—leading to chronic stress, anxiety, and health issues.

I was trapped there, too, fighting unseen battles. It took years to break the cycle, to realise that I was numbing my pain with alcohol and indulgence. I thought this was normal: work hard and play hard. But it wasn't living; I was surviving each day.

Healing began when I addressed unresolved trauma, faced my emotional pain, and paired physical health with emotional well-being. No more quick fixes or self-destructive habits. Just clarity and consistency. I stopped reacting to stress with anger, seeing that it wasn't the world triggering me but the toxins—sugar and alcohol—fuelling the cycle.

When I removed alcohol, sugar and processed from my life, everything changed. I saw the world with new eyes—calm, clear, and capable. You can experience this transformation, too. Don't spend years searching for answers. Let go of the substances holding you back and embrace a life of clarity.

You have a chance to thrive, to wake up energised and focused, and to ask yourself, "What do I truly want in life?" The answers have always been simple.

I believe in you. The best version of you is waiting.

THE DESIRED STATE

For decades, I chased an undefined state, seeking fulfilment in quick fixes—alcohol to numb the day, chocolate for a rush, fleeting pleasure, new possessions, or the temporary high of success. Each felt good momentarily but left the same emptiness behind. I believe this is the void people often feel. What I was longing for was deeper: true healing and resolution. A life where your body is at its best, your mind clear, and your spirit free. A life where you can indeed be yourself.

I didn't realise that the high wasn't leading me anywhere meaningful. Money, successes, indulgences—they fill the void for a moment but fade quickly, leaving you lower than before.

So, what is the state you're genuinely seeking? What could life look like if you committed to change?

It took me decades, but I found it: **feeling calm, having clarity, and being consistent**. When I wake up, I feel light, hopeful, and positive. I live a life where I'm steady, unshaken by chaos, and free from addictive pulls and emotional reactions.

Peace comes when meditation, walking, journaling, nutrition, gym training, and intentional actions are balanced. There is no rush, no hunger for more—just being. The state is calm, clear, and consistent.

But even in this state, it only takes a moment to slip. Sugar, for example, is a silent disruptor. One piece of chocolate can turn into a binge, an endless search for more. It's the cycle of addiction masked as a "treat." One glass of wine leads to a bottle, and soon, the craving returns day after day.

Freedom is breaking this loop. It's finding a place where you crave the healthy, where your body and mind naturally seek what's best for you—nutrition, movement, mindfulness, and peace.

True freedom is a life without cravings or feelings of want, where happiness isn't a quick hit but a steady, enduring calm. That is where absolute freedom lies, and you feel beautiful inside.

INITIAL DISCOMFORT AND RESISTANCE

The dream I've shared is absolute, but so is the discomfort that comes with change. As you start facing your past, it may feel overwhelming, and I'm sorry. But understand this: actual change begins with discomfort. You're not worse off—you're just becoming aware of the challenges you need to address, and that's progress.

The future you want—free from emotional eating, smoking, excessive drinking, or constant highs—requires introspective work. It won't be easy, and it won't happen overnight. I know from experience that giving up alcohol for a month only to return to old habits taught me that real, lasting change takes time. And this isn't about giving things up forever—it's about creating fundamental shifts in how you feel and live daily.

The odds are in your favour of success.

Research indicates that the following are the top factors that contribute to individuals discontinuing new positive habits:

- **Unrealistic Goals**: Setting overly ambitious targets can lead to discouragement. A 2014 survey found that 35% of participants who failed to maintain their New Year's resolutions admitted their goals were unrealistic. **65% were successful**.
- **Lack of Progress Tracking**: Staying motivated without monitoring is challenging. The same survey reported that 33% of individuals did not keep track of their progress, contributing to habit discontinuation. **67% were successful.**
- **Forgetting Commitments**: Busy lifestyles can cause people to forget their new habits. Approximately 23% of respondents in the

survey mentioned forgetting as a reason for not continuing their resolutions. **77% were successful.**

Now you know what doesn't work, addressing these challenges by setting realistic goals, tracking progress, focusing on one habit at a time, and modifying environmental cues can enhance the likelihood of sustaining new positive habits.

What we're building here is a sense of daily contentment and well-being. It's not about your bank balance or job satisfaction. It's about waking up and feeling good, meditating and finding peace, or sitting in silence and feeling whole.

None of these struggles are your fault. Global companies design products—whether it's food, alcohol, or other substances—to be almost irresistible, making habits like drinking or unhealthy eating incredibly hard to control. It took me years to realise that alcohol wasn't helping me; it was holding me back. If you're starting to see this for yourself, take heart—you're not at rock bottom; you're stepping onto the path to a better life.

I promise you that this journey is worth it. Today, I live free from addictions, self-sabotage, and destructive habits. Over time, I moved past them and now feel confident, fulfilled, and alive. I had to face the hard truth, which took decades, but the growth was finally worth every step to feel good and positive.

Give yourself time and grace. This journey is yours alone, and there's no race. Whether it takes weeks, months, or years, know that you're investing in a life that's genuinely yours. The transformation is worth it.

Take a moment to reflect and write in your journal:

- What do you truly want for your future?
- What's holding you back?
- Are you committed to change?

▶ What's the first small step you can take today?

You have the potential to create something unique with your one precious life. Don't let this opportunity pass.

Summary

Small, consistent changes build lasting habits. As James Clear's *Atomic Habits explains*, tiny behavioural shifts—like starting with a short daily walk—compound over time to create meaningful change. Sustainable habits start simple and gradually grow into natural parts of your routine.

Harmful habits, on the other hand, are compounded and destructive. Stress triggers cycles of self-destructive behaviour, such as turning to alcohol, smoking or junk food for relief. Understanding these patterns, often rooted in past issues, is critical to breaking free.

Developing healthy responses to stress, like walking or meditating, can offer relief without the negative consequences. By recognising stress triggers and choosing positive actions, you take control of your responses and break harmful cycles.

The journey begins with awareness, a pause, and the choice to act differently. We are embarking on an objective, life-changing change.

CHAPTER 5
WHAT'S HOLDING YOU BACK FROM FEELING YOUR BEST?

> "The things we reach for in the moment of emotional relief, when repeated often, become the problem, not the solution."

In this chapter, we'll examine the five most common substances people use to relieve stress so you can begin to identify and address them in your journey toward well-being.

ULTRA-PROCESSED JUNK FOOD AND SUGAR

Ultra-processed foods, junk food, and sugar dominate modern diets across the globe, often marketed as quick, convenient, and enjoyable options. These foods are highly processed, losing their original nutritional value and filled with additives, preservatives, and artificial flavours. According to recent statistics, ultra-processed foods comprise approximately 58% of daily calorie intake in the United States and 50% in the UK. This widespread consumption is not limited to Western countries; sales and consumption are also rising in developing nations, contributing to global health issues. Despite their popularity, these foods offer minimal nutritional benefits and come with serious health risks.

One of the primary concerns with ultra-processed foods is their high sugar content. Sugar enhances taste and triggers the brain's reward system, leading to addictive cycles of craving and overconsumption. Globally, sugar consumption has surged, with the average person consuming 24 kilograms (53 pounds) of sugar annually. This figure is even higher in countries like the United States, where the average person consumes approximately 57 kilograms (126 pounds) of sugar yearly. These high levels of sugar intake make it difficult to control food consumption, leading to energy-dense but nutrient-poor diets.

The impact on body weight and obesity rates is striking. The global obesity rate has nearly tripled since 1975, and today, more than 1.9 billion adults are overweight, with 650 million classified as obese. Ultra-processed and sugary foods are significant factors contributing to these numbers. In the United States, over 40% of adults are obese, while the UK reports nearly 28% of adults as obese. These alarming statistics underscore how calorie-rich but nutritionally empty foods contribute to unhealthy weight gain, increasing the risk of severe health issues such as type 2 diabetes, heart disease, and certain types of cancer.

Ultra-processed and junk foods contribute not only to weight gain but also to poor metabolic health. The regular consumption of these foods can lead to insulin resistance, a precursor to type 2 diabetes that affects an estimated 422 million people worldwide. Additionally, these foods contribute to chronic inflammation in the body and cause cardiovascular disease—the leading cause of death globally, responsible for nearly **18 million deaths per year**. The combination of high sugar, unhealthy fats, and artificial additives places undue stress on the body, affecting organs and tissues over time.

The impact extends beyond physical health, affecting mental well-being as well. Studies have shown that diets high in ultra-processed foods and sugar are associated with a higher risk of anxiety and depression. For instance, research indicates that individuals who consume large amounts of processed foods are 40% more likely to experience depression than those who eat a diet rich in whole, unprocessed foods. The causes are due in part to the energy spikes and crashes created by sugar, which can lead to mood swings, irritability, and long-term mental health issues.

It's essential to recognise that these foods are not just lacking in nutrition; they actively harm the body by promoting weight gain, obesity, and associated diseases. Unlike whole, nutrient-dense foods, ultra-processed products offer empty calories, leading to energy imbalances and poor health outcomes. Understanding the scope of this issue is the first step toward making healthier choices and reducing the global burden of diet-related illnesses.

ALCOHOL

Alcohol is a chemical substance classified as a depressant, often consumed for recreational and social purposes. Its main component, ethanol, impacts the central nervous system, slowing brain function and impairing cognitive and motor abilities. While moderate consumption is considered socially acceptable (and often expected) in many cultures, alcohol is inherently toxic and carries significant risks when used regularly or excessively.

Globally, alcohol consumption is widespread, with approximately 2.3 billion people aged 15 and older drinking regularly. Statistics show that men are more likely to consume alcohol than women, with 58% of men and 29% of women reporting alcohol use, reflecting not only a cultural norm but also a deeply ingrained aspect of social interaction and leisure worldwide.

Alcohol is responsible for substantial public health issues. The World Health Organization estimates that alcohol contributes to over **3 million deaths annually**, representing nearly 5% of all global deaths. These figures highlight the scale of its impact, making it a major preventable cause of death and disease.

The health implications of regular or heavy alcohol consumption are severe. Alcohol causes over 200 different medical conditions, including liver disease, heart disease, pancreatitis, and several types of cancer. Long-term use can also lead to neurological damage and cognitive decline, impacting memory and decision-making abilities.

Beyond physical health, alcohol significantly affects mental health. Chronic alcohol use can exacerbate anxiety, depression, and stress disorders. It disrupts the brain's chemical balance, leading to changes in mood and behaviour. Alcohol dependence can also result in alcohol use disorder, a condition that affects approximately 283 million people worldwide.

Despite its social acceptance, alcohol is a highly addictive substance that can impair judgment, disrupt relationships, and reduce overall quality of life. The temporary "feel-good" effect of alcohol is short-lived and often leads to repeated use, creating a cycle of dependence that is difficult to break. This addiction can lead to risky behaviours, poor decision-making, and long-term consequences for both individuals and society.

The economic burden of alcohol-related health issues is immense, costing billions in healthcare and lost productivity annually. As a result, understanding alcohol's true nature, its global use, and its widespread consequences is vital for recognising the serious public health challenge it poses. Efforts to educate people on the risks and provide resources for reducing consumption can be crucial in mitigating its negative impact.

EATING OR DRINKING YOUR EMOTIONS

Emotional eating and emotional drinking are everyday coping mechanisms that people use to deal with stress, sadness, anxiety, or boredom. These behaviours are not due to hunger or the need for sustenance but by the desire to suppress or soothe difficult emotions. The problem with emotional eating and drinking is that they offer only temporary relief, masking underlying issues without resolving them. Instead, they often lead to guilt, regret, and a cycle of dependency that can be difficult to break.

At its core, emotional eating involves consuming food as a response to feelings rather than physical hunger. This behaviour is aligned with cravings for comfort foods high in sugar, fat, or salt, providing a quick but fleeting sense of satisfaction. However, emotional eating can disrupt the body's natural hunger and fullness cues, leading to overeating and long-term issues like weight gain and obesity. The immediate pleasure fades quickly, leaving behind a sense of guilt and self-reproach that compounds emotional stress.

Emotional drinking shares similar patterns. While moderate alcohol consumption is socially accepted, using alcohol to cope with emotions can become problematic. People often turn to alcohol to numb feelings of stress, sadness, or loneliness, creating a temporary sense of relief. However, alcohol is a depressant, and over time, it exacerbates feelings of anxiety and depression rather than alleviating them. Emotional drinking can lead to dependence, where the body starts craving alcohol to manage emotional states, creating a destructive cycle that impacts physical and mental health.

Both emotional eating and drinking have much deeper psychological triggers. These behaviours often stem from a learned response to stress or emotional pain. For many, food and alcohol are associated with comfort, celebration, or relief, so turning to them during difficult times feels natural. This conditioned response can begin early in life and become ingrained, making it challenging to differentiate between genuine needs and emotional urges.

The impact of emotional eating and drinking on the body and mind is significant. Emotional eating often leads to weight gain, increased body fat, and metabolic issues like insulin resistance, raising the risk for type 2 diabetes and cardiovascular diseases. Emotional drinking carries risks such as liver damage, high blood pressure, weakened immune function, and increased chances of developing alcohol use disorder. Both behaviours can also trigger feelings of low self-esteem and shame, reinforcing a cycle where the behaviour becomes both a cause and Consequence of emotional distress.

Breaking the cycle of emotional eating and drinking requires self-awareness and deliberate action. Recognising triggers—stress at work, personal relationship challenges, or loneliness—is essential for developing healthier coping strategies. Techniques such as mindfulness, journaling, and engaging in physical activities can help shift the focus from suppressing emotions to addressing and managing them more constructively. Building a support system through friends, family, or professional guidance can also be vital to recovery.

Understanding hunger and emotional triggers is essential in addressing emotional eating and drinking. Practising mindful eating, where you pay close attention to your hunger cues and emotional state before eating or drinking, can help you distinguish between physical needs and emotional cravings. Similarly, developing healthy routines, such as preparing nutritious meals and practising moderation in social drinking, can reduce reliance on food and alcohol as emotional crutches.

Lastly, embracing self-compassion is critical. Emotional eating and drinking often trigger never-ending cycles of stress, guilt, and shame. Breaking free from these patterns involves recognising that setbacks are part of the journey, and that progress takes time. Practising self-kindness, celebrating small victories, and focusing on gradual change can help replace destructive habits with healthier, more sustainable behaviours that enhance physical and emotional well-being.

TOBACCO AND NICOTINE

Tobacco and nicotine continue to be significant global health concerns despite decades of public health efforts aimed at reducing their use. Tobacco products, including cigarettes, cigars, and smokeless tobacco, contain nicotine, an addictive substance that hooks users and makes quitting difficult.

Currently, there are approximately 1.3 billion tobacco users worldwide, with smoking being the most common form of tobacco consumption. Although smoking rates have declined in many high-income countries due to awareness campaigns and regulations, rates remain high in developing regions, posing ongoing public health challenges.

The health impact of tobacco use is severe. Tobacco is the leading cause of preventable death globally, responsible for more than **8 million deaths each year**, including over 1.2 million non-smokers who die from second-hand smoke exposure. Smoking damages nearly every organ in the body and is linked to a range of health conditions, including heart disease, stroke, chronic obstructive pulmonary disease (COPD), and various forms of cancer, particularly lung cancer, which accounts for more than two-thirds of all smoking-related cancer deaths.

Nicotine, the addictive component of tobacco, is what keeps users hooked. When inhaled or ingested, nicotine rapidly reaches the brain, triggering the release of dopamine and creating a temporary sense of pleasure and relaxation. This effect reinforces the desire to continue smoking or using tobacco products, making it difficult to quit. Over time, the brain adjusts to the regular influx of nicotine, requiring larger doses to achieve the same effect and further deepening the cycle of addiction.

The economic cost of tobacco use is staggering. Globally, it costs the world economy more than $1.4 trillion annually in healthcare expenses and lost productivity, which accounts for nearly 2% of the world's total economic output. Countries with high rates of tobacco use bear significant healthcare burdens, as treating tobacco-related diseases places immense strain on medical systems. This financial impact underscores the urgent need for continued education, prevention, and cessation support programs.

Smoking Tobacco contributes to a range of non-communicable diseases (NCDs), which are the leading cause of death globally. The World Health Organization reports that smoking is responsible for 30% of all cancer deaths and 20% of deaths from cardiovascular disease. The toxic chemicals found in tobacco smoke—more than 7,000, including harmful hundreds and at least 70 known to cause cancer—cause damage that is often irreversible, leading to chronic health conditions and premature death.

The introduction of alternatives like e-cigarettes and vaping devices has complicated public health efforts. While they are sold as safer than traditional tobacco products, research indicates that they are not risk-free. E-cigarettes still contain nicotine and can lead to nicotine addiction, especially among young people, as the appealing flavours and marketing have attracted a new generation of users. Although some studies suggest vaping may be less harmful than smoking cigarettes, the long-term effects remain uncertain, and there is growing evidence of health risks associated with vaping, including lung damage and cardiovascular issues.

Quitting tobacco is difficult due to nicotine's addictive nature, but it is possible with the proper support. Resources such as counselling, nicotine replacement therapy, and prescription medications can double or triple the chances of successfully quitting. Public health initiatives, such as smoke-free policies, taxation, and advertising bans, have effectively reduced tobacco use worldwide. Taking the step to stop or reduce tobacco use not only improves personal health but also contributes to a broader effort to combat one of the leading causes of preventable death worldwide.

RECREATIONAL DRUGS

Recreational drug use is a complex and growing global issue. These include cannabis, cocaine, MDMA (ecstasy), amphetamines, hallucinogens like LSD, and opioids. While each of these drugs has distinct effects on the brain and body, they share a common thread: their potential for addiction, health deterioration, and socio-economic impact. The World Drug Report estimates that over 275 million people worldwide have used drugs in the past year, highlighting the prevalence of recreational drug use and its significant implications.

One of the primary concerns with recreational drugs is their effect on the brain's reward system. Many drugs stimulate dopamine release, producing a temporary euphoria or pleasure. This "high" reinforces the desire to use the drug again, creating a cycle of repeated use that can lead to addiction. Over time, the brain adapts to these repeated dopamine surges, requiring higher doses to achieve the same effect and deepening the cycle of dependence.

The health risks associated with recreational drugs vary depending on the substance, frequency of use, and method of administration. For example, regular cannabis use impaired cognitive function and mental health disorders, including anxiety and depression. Cocaine and amphetamines can lead to cardiovascular problems, severe weight loss, and neurological damage. Opioids, such as heroin and synthetic drugs like fentanyl, are particularly concerning due to their high potential for overdose, which can result in respiratory failure and death. In 2020 alone, there were over 61,000 opioid overdose deaths in the United States, showcasing the deadly consequences of drug misuse.

The impact of recreational drugs extends beyond the individual, affecting families, communities, and society at large. Drug dependence can lead to strained relationships, job loss, and financial instability, creating a ripple effect that exacerbates social issues like poverty and crime. Additionally, the illicit drug trade fuels organised crime and violence, posing significant challenges to law enforcement and public safety in many regions.

Chronic use of recreational drugs aligns with a wide array of health conditions. Long-term stimulant use, such as cocaine and methamphetamine, can result in severe heart problems, liver damage, and mental health disorders. Opioid use carries risks of chronic pain, severe gastrointestinal issues, and immune system suppression.

The economic burden of recreational drug use is substantial, costing global healthcare systems billions each year. The societal impact is similarly significant, with governments and organisations expending resources on prevention, treatment, and law enforcement. According to the United Nations Office on Drugs and Crime (UNODC), drug use costs society more than $600 billion annually in the United States alone, which includes healthcare, lost productivity, and criminal justice expenses.

Efforts to address the issue of recreational drug use require a multifaceted approach that includes prevention, education, and treatment. Harm reduction strategies, such as supervised injection sites and needle exchange programs, aim to reduce the risks associated with drug use. Public health campaigns that educate about the dangers of drug use and its long-term consequences are essential in curbing the prevalence of recreational drug consumption. Additionally, access to treatment programs that offer counselling, medical support, and social rehabilitation is crucial for helping individuals recover and reintegrate into society.

Despite the challenges, there is hope. Advances in addiction treatment, such as medication-assisted therapy (MAT) and cognitive behavioural therapy (CBT), have shown promise in helping individuals overcome drug dependence. Recovery is a journey that requires support, resources, and commitment, but individuals can break free from the cycle of recreational drug use and lead healthier, more fulfilling lives.

LIFE'S PARADOXES

Breaking the cycle of substance use has revealed to me one of life's greatest paradoxes: **the things you turn to for stress relief become the source of your stress.** Whether it's alcohol, junk food, smoking, or getting high, these quick fixes provide temporary relief but come with negative consequences—cravings, guilt, anxiety, and physical discomfort. Over time, they create a vicious loop where the short-term solution becomes a long-term problem.

Abstaining from these substances allows your body and mind to reset. Without the artificial highs and crashes from alcohol, nicotine, junk food, or drugs, your brain's chemistry begins to stabilise, leading to balanced emotional responses and a calmer nervous system. Over time, your natural well-being returns, reducing anxiety and promoting peace. When cared for, the body will naturally feel good—modern life and its dependencies have obscured this natural state.

The reality is harsh: industries profiting from these dependencies are often billion-dollar enterprises built on selling 'happiness' or 'relief' in a bottle, preying on vulnerability and fostering reliance. This is systemic, ingrained in the fabric of our modern world. The truth? You don't need these substances to feel good. The promise of relief they sell is a lie.

The real opportunity lies in moving beyond these short-lived dopamine hits to a state where you feel good naturally and consistently. With time and abstinence, your body can recover, detoxify, and rebuild. Your brain finds balance, emotional regulation improves, and overall well-being improves.

/// WHAT'S HOLDING YOU BACK FROM FEELING YOUR BEST?

This chart shows the stages of substance abstinence to achieving a natural state of calm.

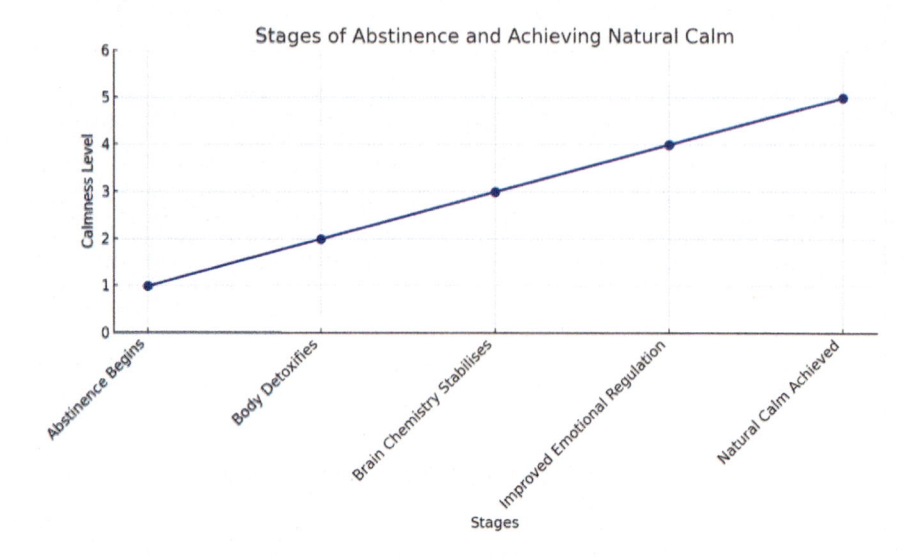

Stages of Abstinence and Achieving Natural Calm

A line chart with "Calmness Level" on the y-axis (0 to 6) and "Stages" on the x-axis, showing a steadily increasing line through the following points:
- Abstinence Begins: 1
- Body Detoxifies: 2
- Brain Chemistry Stabilises: 3
- Improved Emotional Regulation: 4
- Natural Calm Achieved: 5

Your body begins to detox, stabilising brain chemistry, and enhancing emotional regulation—all leading to a steady state of calm and improved well-being. By breaking the cycle and allowing your body to recover, you unlock a better, more balanced version of yourself.

You've been holding yourself back by seeking relief from substances. Give your body the chance to heal and recover, and you will discover that true, lasting well-being has been within you all along.

ONE DAY AT A TIME

We've covered significant information, and I appreciate that these changes can feel overwhelming. Be patient with yourself and take things one day at a time. If you're genuinely absorbing my insights, this could be a pivotal moment for you. It took me decades to reach this stage, and I navigated it alone. You have this book and my experience to guide you, showing that a better, stronger version of yourself is within reach.

Let me introduce you to the "one day at a time" principle—a simple yet powerful approach to change. This mindset helps you focus on the present when the journey feels daunting. Whether cutting out alcohol, sugar, ultra-processed foods or building healthier habits, focusing on today's actions makes the process more manageable. Instead of being overwhelmed by long-term goals, you concentrate on what you can do now or today.

Breaking down change into daily steps reduces stress and makes the journey feel achievable. You don't have to worry about maintaining changes for months or years; take it one day at a time. This approach is beneficial for lifestyle changes requiring discipline, like giving up addictive substances or overhauling your diet. Each small effort adds up over time, and focusing on today helps you build momentum.

Consistency is the cornerstone of success, and this principle supports that by encouraging daily progress. Each day, you choose to avoid unhealthy food, skip a drink, or take a walk. These small daily wins accumulate and turn into significant achievements. By focusing on today, you create a strong foundation that supports future growth.

This approach also fosters self-compassion, which is essential during change. Setbacks happen, and that's okay. The "one day at a time" mindset makes it easier to forgive yourself for a slip and start fresh the next day. Instead of being discouraged by long-term expectations, you focus on doing your best now, allowing room for gradual improvement.

Ultimately, "one day at a time" helps you transform your life by reducing overwhelm and empowering you to stay present. Your daily efforts add up, leading to lasting changes in your physical and emotional health. By staying focused on manageable steps, you set yourself up for success without the pressure of long-term goals weighing you down.

SUMMARY OF YOUR MIND

We've covered so much together, and I want to acknowledge your progress and resilience. My aim has always been to guide you through conquering your inner struggles and moving toward a better you.

I hope you've begun incorporating daily self-care practices like journaling, walking, and meditation and are becoming more aware of how substances impact your emotional well-being. By changing your habits and committing to self-care routines that support your mind and body, you'll feel better over time, experience less stress, and naturally reduce your reliance on substances. Changing your daily actions will help you look and feel healthier. Consistency is the key to lasting improvement.

Journaling each day helps you release emotions rather than letting them fester and lead to destructive behaviours like drinking, smoking, or emotional eating. Choose a journal that prompts you with questions to help you better understand your feelings. Walking daily, aiming for an optimal 10k steps, boosts your physical and mental well-being. Meditation, even for just 10 minutes a day, will enhance mindfulness and inner calm.

I hope you've also spoken with a professional and explored your inner child and past experiences. This deep, introspective work takes time but is worth every moment. It brings healing, peace, and the foundation for a brighter future. Remember, *"Wherever you go, there you are."* You cannot escape being you, so rather than numbing your thoughts and emotions, embrace them. Understand why you feel restless or frustrated, identify the void, and learn how to fill it from within without relying on external crutches.

I appreciate you for embarking on this journey and actively changing your life. The people around you want the best for you, and so do I. Most importantly, you want the best for yourself. You're making meaningful progress and transforming your life one day at a time.

I am proud of you. Keep going.

SECTION 02
YOUR BODY

An Important Message

While we touched on food and emotional eating in Chapter 5, we need to dive deeper now, as this issue may affect you more than you realise. Awareness and understanding are crucial for meaningful change.

This chapter may evoke strong emotions when discussing sensitive body image and food topics. These are deeply personal and complex issues, often overwhelming and without clear solutions. I see and respect your effort if you've struggled and tried countless approaches. I understand because I've been there, battling these challenges for decades.

I want to stress the importance of seeking professional support, such as from a therapist, to explore your relationship with food. Your relationship with food goes beyond what a personal trainer can offer. It delves into understanding why food acts as a 'reward' or 'comfort' and why emotional eating or overeating happens for you.

The struggle with food often runs deeper than simple eating habits, frequently tied to emotional issues rooted in early life experiences. I introduced this idea earlier in the book, so I encourage you to revisit that section or work alongside a therapist as we go through practical guidance for losing weight and improving well-being.

Turning to food in times of stress is often not about physical hunger but soothing an emotional void. The void you feel can be linked to unresolved childhood pain or complicated relationships, areas worth exploring as you move forward on this journey.

Understanding these deeper connections is the key to breaking free from the cycle of emotional eating. With this awareness, support, and practical steps, you can move toward a healthier and more balanced relationship with food.

Introduction to your body

In this section, we'll shift our focus to your body. The mind and body are deeply interconnected, and building mental strength leads to building a better body, creating a growth cycle—and vice versa. This chapter centres on nurturing your body and will cover essential topics such as the food industry, weight loss, and movement.

Reflecting on the future, did you consider how you envision your body in the years to come? Did you include that in your vision?

Health is always my top priority—before family or any other aspect of life. Without health, everything else falls apart. Health is the foundation for living well and feeling good right now. It's a win-win situation.

Review these questions: What do you truly desire for your body regarding how it looks and feels? Can you picture it clearly in your mind? How would having your ideal body affect your life, confidence, and self-respect? Would you feel proud of it and take care of it diligently?

Close your eyes and reflect for a moment. Better yet, journal, walk, or meditate to think deeply about what you genuinely want. Remember, only you know what's suitable for your body and health.

You are in control of your life and your health. Let's consider and decide what you truly want and understand what you might have been suppressing all this time.

THE MIRROR AND THE MARKET

Standing in front of the mirror, ask yourself: are you happy with what you see? For many, the answer is "no," often tied to the desire for weight loss and better health. Your inner conflict arises: "I want to enjoy life and indulge in food, but I also want to lose weight and look better." It feels like an impossible battle.

I understand this struggle—it's been a source of my discontent and unhappiness for years.

Many of us face a constant tug-of-war between the desire for comfort foods and the goal of losing weight. Surveys show that a significant number of people are dissatisfied with their bodies. The Dove Global Beauty and Confidence Report found that 69% of women feel pressured to look beautiful, and a YouGov survey noted that 48% of U.K. adults are unhappy with their appearance. In the U.S., over 80% of women and 40% of men report body dissatisfaction at some point in their lives.

I shared this information earlier, but it's so shocking I want to reiterate the point. The World Health Organization (WHO) estimates that over 1.9 billion adults are overweight, and of these, more than 650 million are obese. 39% of adults worldwide are overweight, and 13% are obese. If current trends continue, by 2035, **51% of the global population—approximately 4 billion people—could be classified as overweight or obese**, highlighting that the struggle with body weight is not just personal: it's a global crisis.

Why is this happening? Understanding the root causes of this issue is essential. Modern lifestyles include highly processed, calorie-dense, and addictive foods that encourage overconsumption while providing little nutritional value. Paired with sedentary habits, emotional eating, economic challenges, and a lack of nutritional education, this creates a challenging global issue. The reality is that being overweight is not merely an individual challenge—it's a systemic issue driven by powerful marketing and the influence of the food industry.

These industries profit from hyper-palatable, dopamine-triggering foods that create dependency.

Foods high in sugar, fat, and salt—engineered for maximum appeal—stimulate the brain's reward centres much like addictive substances do, leading to overconsumption and, in many cases, a reliance on food for comfort and stress relief rather than nourishment.

Addressing this means recognising that the cycle is **not your fault**. The food industry, worth billions, has spent decades conditioning us to crave what keeps them profitable, not what keeps us healthy. Many people also carry unresolved emotional pain from childhood, which fuels the cycle of emotional eating and over-reliance on these hyper-palatable foods.

My goal is to help you break this cycle. By understanding the addictive nature of these foods and why we turn to them for comfort, you can begin to make meaningful changes. Awareness is the first step. When you're ready, we'll look at replacing these habits with sustainable choices that nourish your body and support your well-being.

THE HEALTH RISK TO YOU

If you are overweight or obese, it's often due to a consistent diet high in processed and addictive foods—rich in sugar, unhealthy fats, salt, and refined carbohydrates. This diet poses significant long-term health risks and contributes to various severe health conditions.

Key Health Concerns from Processed Foods

1. **Obesity**: High-calorie processed foods lead to weight gain and obesity, which increase the risk of chronic diseases like heart disease, type 2 diabetes, and certain cancers.
2. **Type 2 Diabetes**: Diets rich in sugar and refined carbs cause blood sugar spikes, leading to insulin resistance and, over time, type 2 diabetes. This condition raises the risk of heart disease, kidney failure, and nerve damage.
3. **Heart Disease**: Unhealthy fats, high sodium, and excess sugar contribute to heart disease, high cholesterol, and high blood pressure. Heart disease is a leading global cause of death and severely impacts quality of life.
4. **Metabolic Syndrome and Hypertension**: A combination of factors, such as high blood pressure, abdominal fat, and elevated blood sugar, characterise metabolic syndrome, which increases the risk of heart disease, diabetes, and stroke. Excess sodium intake from processed foods contributes to high blood pressure, leading to strokes and kidney damage.
5. **Non-Alcoholic Fatty Liver Disease (NAFLD)**: High sugar intake, especially from fructose, leads to fat accumulation in the

liver, causing NAFLD, which can progress to inflammation, cirrhosis, and liver failure.

6. **Mental Health Issues**: Diets high in sugar and processed foods contribute to emotional issues like depression, anxiety, and mood swings. These foods create addiction-like behaviours and can lead to fatigue and brain fog, exacerbating mental health challenges.
7. **Chronic Inflammation and Hormonal Imbalances**: Processed foods high in sugar and unhealthy fats contribute to chronic inflammation, increasing the risk of arthritis, heart disease, and cancer. They can also disrupt hormone regulation, impacting metabolism, reproductive health, and mood.

I will state this again and again. Processed and addictive foods offer little nutritional value and create dependency, leading to weight gain, chronic disease, and overall poor health. A diet reliant on these foods compromises physical and mental well-being and leads to a cycle that is hard to break. Conversely, a balanced diet rich in whole, unprocessed foods is essential for preventing these health risks and maintaining long-term well-being.

/// WHAT'S HOLDING YOU BACK FROM FEELING YOUR BEST?

YOUR BODY AND YOU

The previous statements may not have been easy to read, but it's a meaningful conversation.

I want the best for you—to live a life free from addiction and constant cravings. Let's break down the critical factors we need to address.

1. Most of your diet might not be real *food*; it could be an addictive substance.
2. You may be using food for emotional comfort or support.
3. You might view food as a reward or treat rather than as nutrition.

Does this resonate with you? Take a moment to journal your thoughts and be patient with yourself. Real change takes time, and that's okay. This journey is yours, and with commitment and effort, you can move forward.

Recognising these patterns is the first step. Simple, actionable steps, with motivation and consistency, can transform your habits and your life. Change is possible, and it's within your reach. While it won't be easy, it will be worth it.

Many people have spent years experimenting with diets, plans, and training methods, only to find that the answers are more straightforward than they imagined. Building a fit, lean, and healthy body doesn't require extreme willpower or complex routines. Instead, it's about forming sustainable habits that become a natural part of your life.

There are no quick fixes, fad diets, or special supplements that will lead to lasting change. Fundamental transformation comes from consistent progress and small, daily habit shifts. Life is a long journey, and short-term solutions won't deliver the results you're looking for. Real change only happens as you grow into a healthier version of yourself.

Becoming healthier can be broken down into clear, simple steps that anyone can follow. There is hope, and you can reach your goals with the proper guidance and commitment. The path to a healthier, stronger, and happier you is possible—let's begin this journey together.

CHAPTER 7
SLEEP

THE FOUNDATION OF A BETTER BODY: SLEEP

Sleep is essential to daily life and critical for physical and mental well-being. It aids tissue repair, immune function, memory consolidation, and emotional regulation. Understanding and improving your sleep can be a transformative step toward better health and recovery, forming a vital foundation for building a stronger body and mind.

Why Sleep Matters

Sleep impacts every primary bodily function:

- **Physical Restoration**: Deep sleep triggers muscle repair and tissue regeneration, supported by the growth hormone release.
- **Cognitive Function**: Sleep improves focus, decision-making, and memory by consolidating information learned during the day.
- **Emotional Regulation**: Adequate sleep reduces mood swings and stress levels, enhancing your ability to handle life's challenges.
- **Immune System**: Quality sleep boosts immune response, helping the body fight infections.
- **Metabolism**: Sleep regulates hormones like ghrelin and leptin, affecting hunger, appetite and weight management.

THE CRITICAL ROLE OF CIRCADIAN RHYTHM

Your body's internal 24-hour clock, or circadian rhythm, guides sleep-wake cycles and many other bodily processes. Sleep is regulated by exposure to light, which plays a vital role in managing energy levels, hormone production, and digestion. Disruptions to this natural cycle—such as excessive screen time or irregular sleep patterns—can significantly affect sleep quality and overall health.

Scientific Evidence on Sleep

The research underscores the profound impact of sleep on performance:

- **Cognitive Function**: Sleep deprivation (less than six hours) can slow reaction time by 20-32%, comparable to intoxication, and reduce memory retention by up to 20%.
- **Athletic Performance**: Athletes who sleep 7-9 hours perform better, with improved strength, reaction time, and injury recovery.
- **Productivity**: Sleep-deprived individuals face a 400% increase in attention lapses. Sleep deficits cost the U.S. economy $63 billion annually due to lost productivity.
- **Mental Health**: Poor sleep increases emotional reactivity by 60% and impairs social interaction by affecting how we interpret facial expressions and empathy.

How to Improve Sleep Quality

1. **Keep a Consistent Schedule**: Go to bed and wake up at the same time daily.
2. **Limit Screen Time**: Avoid blue light from screens at least an hour before bed.

3. **Create a Relaxing Environment**: Use blackout curtains, maintain a cool temperature (15-19°C), and ensure your sleep space is quiet.
4. **Avoid Stimulants**: Limit caffeine and alcohol close to bedtime, as they disrupt sleep cycles.
5. **Develop a Bedtime Routine**: Incorporate calming activities like reading or meditation.

The Impact of Alcohol on Sleep

While alcohol might help you fall asleep initially, it fragments sleep, especially REM stages essential for memory and emotional processing. It also acts as a diuretic, causing frequent waking and dehydration, further impairing sleep quality.

Tips for Shift Workers

1. **Create a Dark Environment**: Use blackout curtains and noise-cancelling tools for daytime sleep.
2. **Control Light Exposure**: Limit light after shifts and use bright lights during work to align with your body's alertness.
3. **Strategic Naps**: Short naps (10-20 minutes) can boost alertness but avoid napping close to main sleep times.

In summary, quality sleep is the foundation for better health and well-being. Improving your sleep habits will make you feel more energised, productive, and capable of pursuing your desired life. Prioritise sleep, and the transformation will follow.

HOW TO LOSE WEIGHT

Immediate Correction: Focus on Fat Loss, Not Weight Loss

When working towards better health and body composition, the goal should be to lose fat, not weight. Losing weight without distinguishing between fat, muscle, and water can lead to muscle loss, reduced metabolism, and poor physical performance. Fat loss preserves lean muscle, leading to a leaner, healthier body and improved metabolic health.

The Real Key: Caloric Deficit

Understanding and achieving a caloric deficit is the most effective way to lose fat. Regardless of their methods, all diets ultimately work by creating a deficit.

What Are Calories? Calories are units of energy obtained from food and drinks. Our bodies use these calories for everything, including breathing and movement.

Different foods contain varying amounts of calories:

- Green salad: <50 calories/bowl
- Medium apple: ~95 calories
- 8oz fillet steak: 450 calories
- 200g family-size chocolate bar: ~1,150 calories
- Large pizza: ~2,400 calories (300 calories/slice)

What Is a Calorie Deficit? A calorie deficit means consuming fewer calories than your body needs to maintain weight. In this state, your body taps into stored fat for energy, leading to fat loss.

Example: If your body requires 2,000 calories daily to maintain weight but consumes 1,800 calories, you're in a 200-calorie deficit.

What Is a Calorie Surplus? A calorie surplus is when you consume more calories than needed, leading to weight gain as the body stores the excess as fat.

Example: If you need 2,000 calories daily but consume 2,200 calories, you're in a 200-calorie surplus.

How to Lose Fat with a Calorie Deficit

1. **Calculate Your Daily Calorie Needs**: Use factors like age, weight, and activity level.
2. **Set a Deficit**: Aim for 200-500 calories below your maintenance level for gradual, sustainable fat loss.
3. **Choose Whole Foods**: Eat salads, fruits, vegetables, lean proteins, and whole grains to stay nourished.

Example Plan: If your maintenance calories are 2,500, eating 2,000 calories creates a 500-calorie deficit, resulting in about 0.5 kg (1 lb) of fat loss per week (as 3,500 calories equals ~0.5 kg of body weight).

The Core Takeaways:

- **Calories** are the energy from food.
- **Calorie deficit** = Fat loss.
- **Calorie surplus** = Weight gain.

Consistent calorie deficits supported by balanced eating and regular exercise are essential for lasting fat loss.

Understanding Maintenance Calories

To help you begin, I've created a guide for average maintenance calorie needs based on age and gender. These numbers highlight why maintaining a healthy balance is crucial and explain the global challenges related to obesity and weight management.

Maintenance Calories by age and gender

Age Range	Male Maintenance Calories	Female Maintenance Calories
18-25	2600	2000
26-35	2500	1900
36-45	2400	1800
46-55	2300	1700
56-65	2200	1600
66+	2100	1500

These averages are meant as a guide and may not be exact due to individual differences in body composition and metabolism. The chart shows that you should consume the specified number of calories to maintain weight and less to create a calorie deficit to lose weight. It highlights why weight loss becomes more challenging with age due to a slowing metabolism, but it's not impossible—the key is to reduce calorie intake.

For Example: As a 43-year-old male, I hypothetically decide to 'reward' myself on the weekend with the following foods:

- **Breakfast (English Breakfast):** 1,200 calories
- **Lunch (Burger & Chips):** 1,500 calories
- **Dinner (Large Pizza):** 2,000 calories
- **5 Beers:** 1,000 calories
- **Total Consumed:** 5,700 calories
- **Calories Burned:** 2,400
- **Surplus:** 3,300 calories

This single day adds about 0.5 kg to body weight. Repeating this weekly or multiple times a week can quickly lead to significant weight gain and, eventually, potential obesity.

Your Starting Point: If you're overweight or obese, consuming fewer calories is essential. You might be surprised at how many calories come from 'bad' foods or substances posing as food, which are addictive and are designed to trick you into eating far more than you need.

Replace these with nutrient-dense whole foods to manage calories and improve health:

Examples:

1. Fruits:

- Blueberries (1 cup): 85 calories
- Strawberries (1 cup): 50 calories
- Banana: 100 calories

2. Vegetables:

- Spinach (1 cup raw): 7 calories
- Broccoli (1 cup chopped): 55 calories

3. Lean Proteins:

- Chicken Breast (100g): 165 calories
- Salmon (100g): 208 calories

4. Whole Grains:

- Quinoa (1 cup cooked): 222 calories
- Brown Rice (1 cup cooked): 218 calories

Key Difference: Processed foods are high in calories and low in nutrition and can trigger addictive cravings. Whole foods are nutrient-rich, lower in calories, and satisfying, preventing overeating.

/// SLEEP

Daily weight in's

Keeping an accurate weight record is a simple but powerful tool for tracking fat loss progress. To ensure the most reliable measurements, it's important to weigh yourself under the same conditions every day. Ideally, this should be first thing in the morning, without any clothing, after using the toilet, and before consuming food or water. Following this routine minimises fluctuations caused by food, hydration, or clothing, giving you a true reflection of your body weight.

Daily weigh-ins offer an objective fact about how your body responds to your efforts. Rather than guessing how you've progressed, the scale gives you a tangible number to work with. Recording this number in a free app like MyFitnessPal helps you track trends over time, allowing you to spot patterns and adjust if necessary. For example, if your weight plateaus, it could be an indicator to tweak your calorie intake or activity levels. By making this a habit, you stay accountable to your goals and build a clear picture of your progress, which can motivate you to keep going.

Get excited each day by what the scales say. Start the day with a positive moment and celebrate the progress you are making. One day at a time, one win at a time.

PLEASE NEVER GO ON A 'DIET' EVER AGAIN

The global diet and weight loss industry is vast and growing, valued at approximately $190 billion in 2023 and projected to reach $391.5 billion by 2032. This growth is driven by increasing health awareness, obesity rates, and a shift toward healthier lifestyles. The surge in demand for products like meal replacements, weight loss supplements, innovative diet plans, and online purchasing fuels this expansion. However, this boom also brings misinformation, confusing the industry.

Why Diets Don't Work:

1. **Short-term Focus**: Most diets are designed to produce quick results rather than long-term change. As a result, after the diet period, eating habits return to their previous state, and body fat is regained.
2. **Restrictive Nature**: Cutting out food groups or heavily restricting calories leads to feelings of deprivation, triggering cravings and binge eating.
3. **Psychological Impact**: Diets promote an unhealthy all-or-nothing mindset, leading to guilt and cycles of restriction and overeating, causing stress and anxiety.
4. **Lack of Personalisation**: One-size-fits-all diets don't consider individual metabolism, lifestyle, or medical needs, causing frustration when they fail.
5. **Unsustainability**: Highly restrictive plans are challenging to maintain over the long term, leading to the inevitable fall off the wagon.

6. **Weight vs. Health**: Many diets prioritise weight loss over overall health, leading to extreme practices compromising nutrition and well-being.

What Works: Sustainable change comes from healthier choices and gradually lowering calorie intake by swapping "bad" calories for "good" ones.

Bad Calories: These come from nutritionally poor, calorie-dense foods with added sugars, unhealthy fats, and artificial additives, often designed to trigger cravings.

Examples include:

- **Sugary Foods**: Sweets, cakes, sugary cereals
- **Processed Carbs**: White bread, chips, flavoured snacks
- **Fast Foods**: Fried items, high-calorie burgers, pizzas with processed toppings
- **Sugary Drinks**: Sodas, sweetened lattes
- **Processed Meats**: Bacon, hot dogs, prepackaged deli items

Good Calories: Nutrient-dense foods with vitamins, minerals, and fibre. Examples include:

- **Proteins**: Steak, Chicken, salmon, lentils, eggs
- **Carbs**: Brown rice, quinoa, vegetables, fruits
- **Healthy Fats**: Olive oil, avocados, nuts, fatty fish

Example Strategy (80/20 Rule): If your current diet consists of 80% "bad" calories, aim to slowly shift this ratio until 80% of your diet comes from whole, nutritious foods:

Week-by-Week Plan:

- **Week 1**: 80% bad, 20% good
- **Week 2**: 70% bad, 30% good

- **Week 3**: 60% bad, 40% good
- **Week 4**: 50% bad, 40% good
- **Week 5:** 40% bad, 60% good
- **Week 6:** 30% bad, 70% good
- **Week 7:** 20% bad, 80% good

During this process, your calorie intake naturally decreases, making initial calorie counting unnecessary. Once you reach 80% nutrient-dense foods, focus on consistency and portion control to reduce calories further until you achieve and maintain a comfortable weight.

This gradual approach promotes sustainable weight loss and long-term health.

Optimal Macronutrient Ratios (once 80% of your diet consists of whole foods):

1. **For Fat Loss**: 40% protein, 30% carbs, 30% fats. Example: A balanced 1,800-calorie diet could include protein from chicken and Greek yoghurt, carbs from vegetables and whole grains, and healthy fats like avocado.
2. **Building Muscle**: 50% carbs, 25% protein, and 25% fats. An Example of a 2,500-calorie plan is protein from lean meats and plant-based sources, carbs from oats and sweet potatoes, and healthy fats from nuts and fish.

Conclusion: What you eat influences your weight, while your exercise routine depends on your body composition. Lasting success comes from adopting sustainable lifestyle changes and prioritising nutrient-dense, natural foods over restrictive diets.

BODY COMPOSITION

Body composition is the breakdown of body weight into fat and lean mass. Fat mass includes essential fat for bodily functions and storage of fat under the skin. Lean mass comprises muscles, bones, and organs critical for strength and health. Unlike weight alone, body composition provides a better indicator of overall health. Reducing fat and increasing muscle boosts metabolism, improves physical performance, and lowers health risks. For optimal health, building muscle and reducing fat is vital.

How to Build Muscle

Both men and women benefit from strength training targeting all major muscle groups.

Here's a guide:

Compound Exercises:

- *Squats*: Legs and glutes (body weight, dumbbells, barbell).
- *Deadlifts*: Hamstrings, glutes, lower back (barbell, dumbbells).
- *Bench Press*: Chest, shoulders, triceps (barbell, dumbbells).
- *Pull-Ups/Lat Pull-Downs*: Back and biceps (assisted machine if needed).
- *Rows*: Upper back and biceps (barbell, dumbbells, cables).

Isolation Exercises:

- *Bicep Curls*: Arm muscles (dumbbells, resistance bands).
- *Tricep Extensions*: Triceps (dumbbells, cables).
- *Lunges*: Legs and glutes (body weight, added weight).
- *Leg Curls/Extensions*: Target hamstrings/quadriceps.

Bodyweight Exercises:

- *Push-Ups*: Chest, shoulders, triceps.
- *Planks*: Core strength.
- *Bodyweight Squats/Lunges*: Lower body strength.
- *Dips*: Triceps and chest (bench or dip station).

Consistency and Progressive Overload:

- Gradually increase weights or reps to build muscle.
- Aim for 3-4 weekly workouts with rest days for recovery.

Protein and Recovery:

- Prioritise protein intake and sleep for muscle repair and growth.

The 2 Phases of Gym Training

Understanding gym training in two phases optimises results:

Phase 1: Fat Loss and Muscle Retention

- **Objective**: Reduce body fat while retaining muscle.
- **Approach**: Caloric deficit (e.g., 2,000-2,200 calories if maintenance is 2,500). Strength training with compound exercises (3-4 sets, 6-10 reps) signals the body to preserve muscle.
- **Diet**: High protein (1.2-1.5 grams/kg body weight). Lean protein sources like chicken, fish, tofu, and legumes are essential.
- **Cardio**: Steady-state or HIIT sessions 2-3 times a week boost calorie burn but should be balanced to avoid muscle loss.

Phase 2: Muscle Building

- **Objective**: Gain muscle mass and strength.

- ▸ **Approach**: Caloric surplus (e.g., 2,800-3,000 calories if maintenance is 2,500). Progressive overload is vital—gradually increase weights or reps.
- ▸ **Diet**: Prioritise carbs (e.g., brown rice, whole grains) to fuel workouts and pair them with protein for recovery. Balance healthy fats (e.g., avocado, nuts) to support hormone health.
- ▸ **Training**: Compound movements with isolation exercises for targeted growth.

Cycles

Cycling between phases (e.g., 4-6 months of muscle building, 2-3 months of fat loss) prevents stagnation and refines body composition.

Patience and Consistency

Results take time. Gradual, sustainable progress ensures muscle growth, fat loss, and long-term health. Tracking workouts and nutrition and focusing on long-term goals helps maintain motivation and adapt strategies effectively. The aim is a balanced fitness approach that supports strength, aesthetics, and health.

THE IMPORTANCE OF CARDIOVASCULAR EXERCISE

Cardio exercises target the heart, lungs, and circulatory system and are crucial for overall health and fitness.

Key benefits include:

- **Improved Heart Health**: Strengthening the heart enables more efficient blood circulation and reduces the risk of heart disease, high blood pressure, and stroke.
- **Enhanced Lung Capacity**: Increases the body's ability to deliver oxygen to muscles, supporting stamina and endurance.
- **Boosts Calorie Burn and Weight Management It** aids in burning calories and supporting weight loss or maintenance, with high-intensity cardio (e.g., HIIT) continuing to burn calories post-exercise.
- **Supports Mental Health**: It releases endorphins, reduces anxiety, depression, and stress, and enhances mood and mental well-being.
- **Improves Circulation**: Promotes healthy blood flow, reducing clot risk and enhancing nutrient and oxygen delivery.
- **Lowers Blood Sugar and Boosts Metabolism**: It helps regulate blood sugar and increases metabolic rate, which benefits those with or at risk of type 2 diabetes.

Cardio exercise supports heart and lung health, mental well-being, weight management, and overall health.

Examples of Cardio Exercises

Cardio can range from low- to high-intensity activities. Walking is a favourite due to its accessibility, fat-burning benefits, and support for muscle retention.

Other practical cardio exercises include:

- **Running/Jogging**: Improves heart health and endurance.
- **Cycling**: Joint-friendly and adjustable in intensity, suitable for all fitness levels.
- **Swimming**: A full-body, low-impact workout that enhances cardiovascular health and muscle strength.
- **Jump Rope**: High-intensity, calorie-burning, and builds coordination.
- **Rowing**: A whole-body workout that boosts cardiovascular endurance and strengthens the core, upper body, and legs.
- **HIIT (High-Intensity Interval Training)** alternates bursts of intense activity with short recovery periods and is customisable to various fitness levels.
- **Walking**: Low impact yet effective for heart health, especially at an increased pace or incline.
- **Dance Workouts (e.g., Zumba)** are fun, engaging, and great for cardiovascular fitness and muscle use.
- **Stair Climbing**: Intense leg and glute workout using stairs or a machine.
- **Kickboxing**: Combines cardio with strength, enhancing coordination and burning calories.

Cardio exercises can be varied in type and intensity, making workouts adaptable, engaging, and effective for maintaining overall fitness and health.

LEARNING TO LOVE EXERCISE

From "I Hated Running" to Marathons: A Journey of Transformation

Let me start with a story. At school, I dreaded running. I was always the slowest, nicknamed 'slow-mo' by the other boys. Football was my passion, but I needed to be faster to be good at it. I accepted that running wasn't for me, leaving me disheartened and resigned.

Fast forward decades to March 2020, when COVID-19 shut down the gyms. With no other fitness options available, I reluctantly gave running another chance. I struggled through a mere 7-minute jog on the first day and felt defeated. But the next day, I pushed for 12 minutes. By day three, I managed 19 minutes, and I was surprised by how quickly my body adapted.

I began listening to podcasts and diving into episodes of Joe Rogan's show and soon found myself running 30-45 minutes each morning. What was once dreadful became something I started to enjoy. The podcasts distracted my mind, helping me slip into a 'flow state' where time passed unnoticed, and the initial discomfort faded away.

One day, I heard an episode featuring David Goggins, the ultramarathon runner and former Navy SEAL known for his incredible resilience and mental toughness. His story lit a fire, pushing me to challenge my limits.

In May 2020, six weeks after starting, I completed 31 half marathons in 31 days, raising £3,500 for the NHS. I even ended the challenge with back-to-back full marathons. It felt surreal, from hating running to running 31 half marathons and consecutive marathons in under three months.

That year, I continued running and completed 74 half-marathons and four marathons. My transformation was profound: I didn't just tolerate running; I grew to love it. What changed? I pushed through those first difficult weeks, and the enjoyment followed.

Rethink Your Mindset on Exercise

If I can flip my perspective on running after a lifetime of avoidance, can I ask you? What are your fixed mindsets about exercise? Maybe you hate walking, but why? Can you challenge that belief? You already walk every day; what if you approached it with intention? Find a great podcast or playlist, lace up, and start. You might look forward to it as some well-earned 'me' time. It is possible; it's just mindset.

You can shift from "I have to do this" to "I get to do this".

The Gratitude Mindset

Imagine suddenly losing your ability to walk due to an accident. Wouldn't you wish to turn back time and savour every step? It's a sobering thought highlighting how we take physical abilities for granted. Embracing gratitude changes how you view exercise—you'd prioritise walking and cherish it.

Many people dread exercise, seeing it as a chore, and never tap into its potential benefits. This mindset holds them back from reaching their health and fitness goals.

My Tips for Loving Exercise

1. **Start Small**: Start with manageable activities like short walks or jogging. Gradually building up will make it easier to form daily habits without overwhelming yourself.
2. **Find What You Enjoy**: Experiment with various activities—swimming, hiking, strength training, yoga, or dance. Once you

find what excites you, aim to repeat it 3-4 times per week and schedule it like any other priority.
3. **Focus on the Feeling**: Notice how you feel during and after exercise—more energised, less stressed, stronger. Focusing on these positives, rather than appearance alone, can boost motivation.
4. **Set Achievable Goals**: Progress fuels motivation. Set small, weekly goals like trying a new workout or hitting a specific step count and celebrate your successes.
5. **Make it Social or Fun**: Exercise with friends, join a class or pair it with enjoyable activities like listening to a podcast or your favourite playlist.

Learning to love exercise takes time, but with the right approach, it becomes something you look forward to. For lasting change, please find what you enjoy, lean into it, and make it part of your life.

THE CRUCIAL ROLE OF FLOW STATE

Understanding Flow State: Your Key to Enjoyable and Sustainable Exercise

Flow state, or being "in the zone," is a powerful mental state where you're fully immersed, focused, and energised by an activity. Time seems to dissolve, and you feel productive and fulfilled. Psychologist Mihály Csíkszentmihályi, who pioneered the study of flow, found it occurs when a task balances challenge with skill.

Characteristics of Flow:

- **Intense Focus**: Total concentration on the task at hand.
- **Loss of Self-Consciousness**: Minimal awareness of yourself or external distractions.
- **Time Distortion**: Time feels like it speeds up or slows down.
- **Effortless Action**: The activity feels engaging and smooth.

Flow happens when an activity is challenging enough to engage you fully but not so complicated that it causes stress. It's common in sports, music, writing, or any creative work that matches your skill and passion.

When I learned to love running, achieving a flow state was a game-changer. I transitioned from hating running to relishing it by reaching a state where I was moving without thinking, fully immersed in the experience. This mindset shift helped me find enjoyment in something I once dreaded.

How to Achieve Flow:

- **Find the Right Challenge**: Choose tasks that push your abilities but are achievable. If a task is too easy, you'll be bored; if it is too hard, you'll feel anxious.
- **Set Clear Goals**: Establish specific, achievable objectives. Instead of "I'll work out," set a goal like, "I'll run for 30 minutes." Clear goals enhance focus and progress.
- **Eliminate Distractions**: Turn off notifications and create a space that supports uninterrupted focus.
- **Focus on the Process**: Embrace the present moment without obsessing over results. For instance, I enjoy being outside, taking in nature, enjoying the fresh air, and taking a break from work.
- **Practice Regularly**: The more often you engage with an activity, the easier it becomes to achieve flow.
- **Seek Immediate Feedback**: To fine-tune your efforts, opt for activities that allow you to gauge progress quickly, like lifting weights or writing.

Flow State and Exercise

Achieving flow during exercise can transform workouts from a chore to an immersive, rewarding experience. When you reach a flow state, you become fully connected with your movements, making workouts enjoyable and less mentally taxing.

How Flow Enhances Exercise:

- **Boosts Performance and Motivation**: Flow helps you tap into peak performance, allowing your mind and body to sync seamlessly for better form, power, and energy. The positive feedback loop encourages you to return for more.

- **Increases Enjoyment**: When exercise feels engaging rather than a task, it fosters a sustainable, long-term commitment to fitness.
- **Reduces Perception of Effort**: Immersion in flow can make physical discomfort feel less daunting, allowing you to push harder and longer with ease.
- **Improves Form**: Deep focus helps maintain technique, enhancing safety and efficiency.
- **Builds Mental Resilience**: Flow teaches you to stay present through challenges, cultivating resilience and mental toughness that carry over to other areas of life.

Achieving Flow in Your Workouts

You can't force a flow state; it emerges naturally when the conditions are right. I often find flow in deep conversations, writing, running and weightlifting—activities I once resisted but grew to love through consistent practice.

Try This: Journal about activities you feel drawn to and consider if you could improve and enjoy them over time. Start experimenting with new activities. You might discover an unexpected passion, as I did with running and writing.

My Tips for Embracing Exercise:

- **Start Small**: Begin with small, manageable activities like walking or light jogging. Build gradually to form a habit.
- **Explore**: Try different activities, such as swimming, yoga, hiking, and strength training. Variety helps you find what resonates.
- **Focus on Feeling**: Pay attention to how exercise makes you feel—energised, relaxed, or strong. Prioritise this over appearance.
- **Set Small Goals**: Weekly goals can build momentum and offer motivation.

- **Add Enjoyment**: Make workouts social or pair them with podcasts or playlists to boost enjoyment.

Loving exercise and reaching a flow state takes time, but it's worth it. Find what you enjoy, be consistent, and let the process unfold. Over time, exercise shifts from "something I have to do" to "something I look forward to doing."

/// SLEEP

WHY HEALTH AND FITNESS IS RENTED

Whatever you choose, you'll pay the price for the rest of your life.

While choosing to do nothing and avoiding investment in health and fitness may seem easier now, the consequences will catch up over time. Refraining from restricting physical activity and wellness leads to a body that becomes less capable, less resilient, and less agile.

Everyday tasks become more challenging, and quality of life diminishes as strength, flexibility, and endurance fade. While ignoring health maintenance might feel convenient, it often results in more significant health issues and limitations down the line.

On the other hand, choosing to invest in your health means paying the "rent" daily through consistent actions like exercise, proper nutrition, stress management, and good sleep.

Viewing health as a rental emphasises that it requires continuous effort. Like maintaining a home, your body thrives when cared for regularly, helping you avoid "eviction" in the form of preventable health setbacks.

Why the "Rented Health" Perspective Matters

Seeing health as a rented state underscores that it's not guaranteed. Just as neglecting rent payments can lead to eviction, failing to maintain health can lead to its decline. This mindset drives smarter choices about food, exercise, rest, and mental well-being, reminding everyone that health needs daily attention and effort. Each favourable decision is an investment that yields long-term benefits, preventing issues and preserving quality of life.

Routine care acts as preventative maintenance for the body. Regular check-ups, balanced nutrition, and an active lifestyle help prevent wear and tear, keeping you strong and capable for years to come. This approach fosters mindfulness about the future, encouraging self-care as an ongoing responsibility rather than an afterthought.

Commitment, Not Perfection

Results take time. One common pitfall is rushing the process, chasing quick fixes like "get ripped in 30 days" or "lose 10kg in 2 weeks." These are not only unrealistic but unhealthy. True transformation comes from slow, consistent effort.

At 43, I've finally found my rhythm after two decades of 'trying' and 'dieting'. While I've experienced results over the years, combining training with proper nutrition has shown me that long-term commitment and slow change yield the most significant rewards. There will be setbacks—falling off the wagon is inevitable. No one is perfect. What matters is how you respond. Each stumble is a chance to start again, stronger and more determined to find a consistent approach.

Every Choice Shapes Your Future

Every moment presents a choice: who are you becoming with each mouthful of food, each step taken, and each minute at the gym? Each action is a vote for or against the future you desire. Your journey won't be linear and will take longer than you want, but you will progress at your rate through resilience and consistent effort.

You're far stronger than you realise. Trust in your ability to take one more step, make a healthier choice, and embrace the process. Your future self will thank you for every vote you cast in its favour.

INVESTING IN A PERSONAL TRAINER: YOUR GUIDE TO LASTING FITNESS SUCCESS

Choosing to prioritise health and fitness is a powerful commitment. To maximise long-term results, consider partnering with a personal trainer. The right trainer provides expertise, motivation, and support tailored to your goals, making your fitness journey more effective and enjoyable.

Why a Personal Trainer? A skilled personal trainer brings structure, accountability, and personalised coaching. They help you stay consistent, avoid common pitfalls, and reduce the risk of injury. With their guidance, you're more likely to achieve and sustain progress. However, finding the right trainer is essential for success.

Key Considerations When Choosing a Trainer:

1. **Qualifications and Certifications**: Ensure your trainer is certified by reputable organisations, which signals training in anatomy, exercise science, and safe methods. Specialised certifications (e.g., weightlifting, sports conditioning, or corrective exercise) can be a bonus, aligning with specific needs or goals. Qualified trainers offer scientifically-backed workout plans that match your experience level and objectives.

2. **Experience**: Experience matters. Trainers with years of hands-on work know how to adapt techniques to fit different clients. Ask about their experience with clients at your fitness level and with your goals (e.g., weight loss, muscle gain, or rehabilitation). Client testimonials or progress photos can give insight into their effectiveness.

3. **Personality and Communication Style**: A great trainer is more than knowledgeable—they're a motivating partner. During an in-

itial consultation, note how they listen, ask questions, and explain their approach. You should feel comfortable and inspired by their energy, as the right dynamic can make workouts more engaging and rewarding.

Questions to Ask a Potential Trainer:

- What certifications do you hold, and how do you stay updated on the latest fitness trends?
- How many years of experience do you have, and have you worked with clients who share my goals?
- Can you provide client testimonials or success stories?
- What is your training philosophy, and how do you tailor workouts to individual needs?
- How do you track progress, and how often will we assess my results?
- What's your approach to nutrition advice, and do you offer guidance in that area?
- How do you handle setbacks or periods where motivation is low?
- What's your availability, and do you offer remote or flexible training options?
- How do you ensure safety and prevent injuries during workouts?

The Benefits of a Personal Trainer:

- **Education and Safety**: Trainers teach proper form, mobility, nutrition, and recovery techniques, reducing the risk of injury and promoting a balanced approach to fitness. This knowledge stays with you, supporting your fitness long after your sessions.
- Structure and Accountability: Knowing someone is waiting for you at the gym boosts motivation and helps maintain a routine. Trainers monitor your progress, adjust your plan as needed, and celebrate your milestones, keeping the journey rewarding and on track.

Final Thoughts: Choosing the right personal trainer can be transformative. With their tailored guidance, motivation, and expertise, you gain a supportive partner who helps you push past limits and achieve sustainable results. The right trainer turns fitness from a solo struggle into an empowering journey, making once-unattainable goals feel within reach.

SUMMARY OF YOUR BODY

Building a Healthier Body and Lifestyle

Shifting the focus from generic weight loss to targeted fat loss is the first step in transforming your health. Unlike weight loss, which can involve the loss of muscle, water, and fat, focusing on fat loss preserves lean muscle, resulting in a toned physique and better metabolic health. Achieving this requires creating a sustainable calorie deficit through mindful eating rather than restrictive dieting. Understanding calories and tracking intake set the stage for long-term success without the frustration of short-lived results.

The Power of Quality Sleep

Sleep is the cornerstone of physical and mental well-being and crucial for recovery, immunity, and emotional stability. The body repairs itself during sleep, and essential brain functions regulate mood and cognition. Establish a consistent schedule and create a calm, restful environment to improve sleep quality. For shift workers, managing light exposure and following a pre-sleep routine can help them adapt to unconventional hours and promote optimal rest.

The Role of Calories and Macronutrient Balance

Understanding your body's energy needs is essential for reaching health and fitness goals, whether fat loss, muscle gain, or maintenance. Prioritising whole, nutrient-dense foods helps control hunger and cravings while providing essential vitamins and minerals. Reducing ultra-processed foods and balancing macronutrients foster consistent energy levels and overall health.

Sustainable Habits Over Quick Fixes

The key to lasting health and fitness is developing sustainable habits and gradually changing. Instead of restrictive diets, incorporate whole foods and practice the 80/20 rule—80% nutrient-dense foods and 20% indulgences. This balanced approach encourages long-term adherence and a positive relationship with food. Finding joy in exercise and shifting to a positive mindset about physical activity boosts consistency and makes workouts more enjoyable and effective.

The Benefits of Waking Up Early

Waking up early can significantly enhance productivity, focus, and mental well-being. Early risers enjoy peaceful, distraction-free mornings, perfect for setting intentions, exercising, or quiet reflection. Cultivating an early wake-up routine can lead to healthier choices throughout the day, creating a positive ripple effect that supports long-term well-being.

A Holistic Approach to Health

Combining these habits—focusing on fat loss, ensuring quality sleep, understanding nutrition, developing sustainable fitness practices, and starting the day early—builds a strong foundation for a healthier, more fulfilling life. Small, consistent changes lead to profound results, fostering a lifestyle where wellness is achievable, enjoyable, and sustainable.

SECTION 03
YOUR MONEY

CHAPTER 8
MONEY IS FREEDOM

Money matters because it is a fundamental tool that provides access to essential resources, choices, and opportunities. While it's not the sole component of a fulfilling life, it lays the groundwork for security and freedom, enabling people to meet their needs, pursue their goals, and navigate challenges effectively. At its essence, money serves as a means of exchange and a store of value, facilitating economic participation, access to necessities such as food, shelter, and healthcare, and investment in education and personal well-being.

Beyond meeting basic needs, money grants the freedom to make choices aligned with personal goals and values. It unlocks opportunities for education, travel, and enriching experiences that broaden perspectives and enhance life's quality. Financial security allows individuals to follow their passions, invest in personal development, and make lifestyle choices that promote mental and physical health. This freedom often translates to a more balanced, fulfilling life, allowing people to prioritise relationships, growth, and self-care.

Money also enables people to plan and build a legacy. Mindful management provides the means to care for loved ones, invest in future generations, and contribute meaningfully to society. Through charitable giving, community support, and creating businesses and jobs, money allows individuals to have a positive impact and support causes they believe in. In this way, it becomes a tool for lasting influence, shaping a better future for oneself and others.

Ultimately, money is only part of it but represents the potential for greater control, stability, and opportunity. It acts as a safety net in times of uncertainty and helps create a life that reflects one's values. By enabling independence, security, and influence, money becomes a powerful catalyst for personal growth, meaningful connections, and a life well-lived.

THE QUIET STRENGTH OF TRUE WEALTH

True wealth is best understood not by outward displays but by the quiet, enduring security it offers. It doesn't need to announce itself through flashy possessions or extravagant gestures. Instead, it resides in the calm assurance of financial stability—a steady foundation built over time that withstands life's changes and challenges. Like a well-tended tree, true wealth grows quietly, setting deep roots and expanding patiently. It is both a state of mind and a solid ground, bringing comfort and peace without needing to be showcased or validated.

The true essence of wealth is freedom—the freedom to make choices without fear, follow passions, and take risks that align with personal values, free from financial desperation.

Wealth allows for a life of purpose and authenticity, untethered from the need to prove one's worth through material markers. Those who understand wealth in this way find its rewards more fulfilling than anything that can be bought or displayed. It's about living fully and freely, showcasing inner richness rather than external excess.

By contrast, loud displays often reflect a desire for validation, an attempt to create an illusion of abundance that may not underpinned by proper stability. While they may draw attention, such displays often mask financial strain or deeper insecurities. True wealth, however, is inwardly satisfying; it needs no audience because its value lies in the security and freedom it brings, not in external approval. Wealth results from mindful choices, strategic planning, and consistent effort. It is intentional, resilient, and capable of weathering life's storms, grounded in substance rather than image.

Wealth is a lifestyle of deliberate choices, responsibility, and a lasting sense of contentment. It isn't about chasing luxury for appearances but about embracing simplicity and understanding that true richness lies in having "enough"—enough security, freedom, and peace of mind. Those who grasp this know that the essence of wealth is to enable a meaningful, fulfilling life. It is a state of quiet power, bringing genuine, lasting satisfaction without the need for external recognition.

THE RICHEST MAN IN BABYLON

The Richest Man in Babylon is a classic book by George S. Clason that imparts timeless financial wisdom through a series of parables set in the ancient city of Babylon. First published in 1926, it became a foundational text for understanding personal finance and wealth-building principles. The book presents lessons and engaging stories illustrating the fundamental concepts of saving, investing, and managing money.

The investment strategy behind *The Richest Man in Babylon* centres on timeless wealth-building principles, emphasising discipline, patience, and prudent decision-making; the book presents these ideas through parables set in ancient Babylon, focusing on how ordinary people can build wealth through straightforward, actionable habits.

Pay Yourself First: The central principle is consistently saving at least 10% of income and setting aside a portion before spending. This habit builds wealth over time, creating a foundation for financial security.

Live Below Your Means: By avoiding unnecessary expenses and living on less than one earns, one can redirect more money into savings and investments, preventing lifestyle inflation from draining potential wealth.

Put Money to Work: Clason advocates investing in ventures that bring reliable, steady returns instead of letting savings sit idle. The point is to invest in stocks, property, or other investments with proven track records and value. The goal is to grow wealth steadily rather than seeking high-risk, quick returns.

Seek Advice from the Wise: Investing is most effective when guided by knowledge and experience, so learning from or consulting those with proven success helps avoid mistakes and enhances results.

Protect Wealth: Risk management is vital. It involves investing only after carefully evaluating their soundness and avoiding get-rich-quick schemes. Clason emphasises protecting wealth through insurance, intelligent choices, and avoiding overly speculative opportunities.

These principles create a disciplined approach to wealth-building, focusing on slow, steady growth rather than rapid gains. The strategy is about developing good habits and making wise, incremental decisions that lead to lasting financial independence.

AN INTRODUCTION TO INVESTING

Investing Made Simple: A Path to Building Wealth

Many people may not fully understand investing or have never considered it. Let's break down what investing is, why it matters, and how it can be a consistent strategy for building wealth over time. Investing is for everyone, regardless of job or income—everyone should protect their future through smart investments.

What Is Investing? Investing means allocating money to assets or ventures to generate future income or profit. Simply, it's using money to make more through growth or income.

How Investing Works:

- **Capital Allocation** involves investing money in assets like stocks, bonds, real estate, or businesses with the expectation that they will grow in value or provide returns.
- **Growth and Compounding**: Investments increase in value through appreciation and compounding, where returns on the initial investment and accumulated gains build wealth over time, creating a "snowball" effect.

Types of Investments:

- **Stocks**: Shares in companies that increase in value over time may pay dividends.
- **Bonds**: Loans to governments or corporations that pay interest, offering steady income with lower risk.

- **Real Estate**: Direct property investments or real estate investment trusts (REITs) that provide rental income and long-term value growth.
- **Mutual Funds/ETFs**: Professionally managed collections of stocks or bonds that simplify diversification.
- **Alternative Investments**: Assets like commodities, cryptocurrencies, or private equity offer diversification but often have higher risk.

Risk and Return:

- **Risk-Reward Balance**: Higher-risk investments, like stocks, offer the potential for higher returns but also greater risk. Lower-risk options, like bonds, provide more stability with lower returns.
- **Diversification**: Spreading investments across different asset types reduces the impact of poor performance in any one asset, stabilising returns.

Investment Strategies:

- **Growth Investing**: Targeting high-growth potential assets, such as tech stocks.
- **Income Investing**: Focusing on investments that provide steady income, like dividend stocks or bonds.
- **Value Investing**: Identifying undervalued assets expected to increase as the market corrects.
- **Long-Term vs. Short-Term**: Long-term strategies leverage the power of compounding over years, while short-term strategies involve frequent trading to capitalise on market changes.

Setting Investment Goals:

- **Financial Goals**: To guide your strategy, define what you're investing for—retirement, buying a home, or generational wealth.
- **Time Horizon**: Your investment duration affects risk levels. Long-term goals can accommodate higher-risk assets, while short-term goals benefit from conservative investments.

Why Invest?

- **Wealth Growth**: Investments generally grow wealth faster than traditional savings accounts.
- **Beating Inflation**: Investments typically yield returns that outpace inflation, preserving and growing purchasing power.
- **Passive Income**: Assets like rental properties, dividend stocks, or bonds provide regular income with minimal active work.

Conclusion: Investing involves thoughtful planning, balancing risk and reward, and maintaining a long-term perspective. With the right strategy, investing can become a robust financial security and growth tool accessible to everyone willing to take the first step.

COMPOUND INTEREST

> "Compound interest is the eighth wonder of the world. He who understands it earns it; he who doesn't pays it." Albert Einstein

Understanding Compounding: The Key to Building Wealth

Compounding is the process by which investments grow over time as the returns earned on the initial amount (the principal) generate additional returns. In simple terms, compounding means earning returns on your returns, creating a powerful snowball effect that accelerates growth significantly over time.

How Compounding Works:

1. **Initial Investment (Principal)**: You start with an initial sum of money.
2. **Earnings on Investment**: The principal earns interest or returns over time.
3. **Reinvesting Returns**: Returns are added to the principal to calculate future earnings on a more extensive base (initial investment + previous returns).
4. **Continued Growth**: This cycle repeats, with each period's earnings added to the principal, increasing the base amount and compounding future growth.

Example of Compounding: Imagine investing £1,000 at an annual growth rate of 10%:

- **Year 1**: 10% of £1,000 is £100, so you now have £1,100.
- **Year 2**: 10% of £1,100 is £110, so you now have £1,210.
- **Year 3**: 10% of £1,210 is £121, so you now have £1,331.

Rather than simply adding £100 each year, the investment grows faster because you're earning returns on both the principal and previous returns.

The Power of Time in Compounding: The impact of compounding grows exponentially over time. The earlier you start investing, the more time your money has to grow, leading to significantly larger returns. An investment compounded over 30 years can grow substantially more than one compounded over 10 years.

Why Compounding Matters:

- **Accelerates Wealth**: Compounding boosts the growth rate of your investments, making it a powerful tool for building wealth.
- **Rewards Early Investing**: Starting 'now' gives your money more time to compound, maximising returns over the long term.
- **Beats Inflation**: Compounded growth helps your investments outpace inflation, preserving and increasing purchasing power.

Summary: Compounding is one of the most effective strategies for growing investments. By harnessing time and reinvested returns, compounding can turn modest investments into significant wealth through exponential growth. Starting early and letting your money work for you over time is the key to taking full advantage of this powerful financial principle.

WHAT ARE LOW-COST ETFS?

Disclaimer: I am not a qualified financial planner. Any guidance or strategies provided are shared for informational and entertainment purposes only.

Understanding Low-Cost ETFs and Their Role in Building Wealth

Investing may seem complex, but it's essential to securing your financial future. Based on decades of research, one effective strategy for consistent wealth-building involves low-cost ETFs (Exchange-Traded Funds). These investments are accessible to everyone, regardless of income or job, and can be an intelligent way to safeguard your future and that of your family.

What Are Low-Cost ETFs? A low-cost ETF is an investment fund that pools money from many investors to buy a diversified portfolio of assets, such as stocks or bonds and trades on stock exchanges. The "low-cost" aspect comes from reduced management fees and expenses compared to actively managed funds.

Characteristics of Low-Cost ETFs:

- **Passive Management**: Most low-cost ETFs aim to track a specific market index (e.g., the S&P 500), which keeps costs low.
- **Low Expense Ratios**: Typically, between 0.1% and 0.3%, meaning minimal fees relative to your investment.
- **Diversification**: Provides broad exposure to various assets in a single fund, spreading risk.
- **Liquidity and Flexibility**: ETFs trade throughout the day, such as stocks, offering greater flexibility.

Why Choose Low-Cost ETFs?

- **Cost Efficiency**: Lower fees mean you retain more returns over time.
- **Market Exposure**: Easy access to entire market indices, allowing you to follow broad market trends.
- **Tax Efficiency**: Generally, more tax-efficient than mutual funds, potentially reducing capital gains taxes.

Popular Low-Cost ETFs:

- **Vanguard S&P 500 ETF (VOO)**: Tracks the S&P 500 with an expense ratio of 0.03%.
- **iShares Core MSCI World ETF (IWDA)**: Covers developed market stocks with a low expense ratio.
- **Schwab U.S. Broad Market ETF (SCHB)**: Offers exposure to the entire U.S. stock market at a minimal cost.

Why the S&P 500? An S&P 500 ETF tracks the performance of 500 leading U.S. companies across diverse sectors, such as technology, healthcare, and finance. This index is the benchmark for the overall U.S. stock market.

Key Features of S&P 500 ETFs:

- **Diversification**: Investing in an S&P 500 ETF exposes you to various large-cap companies across multiple sectors.
- **Low Cost**: Top ETFs like VOO, SPY, and IVV have expense ratios as low as 0.03% to 0.10%.
- **Historical Returns**: The S&P 500 has averaged annual returns of around 10% over the long term, though this includes periods of volatility and downturns.

The Power of Compounding: Compounding means earning returns on your returns, accelerating growth over time. For example, a 10% average annual return can double your investment roughly every seven years, significantly building wealth if left to grow over decades.

Expected Returns and Considerations:

- **Long-Term Growth**: This option is ideal for investors with a time horizon of 10+ years, aligning with historical average returns of around 10% per year.
- **Inflation Adjustment**: After inflation, the average annual return is closer to 7%, a strong return for long-term growth with minimal risk.
- **Market Volatility**: Be prepared for periodic downturns, as long-term gains come with short-term fluctuations.

Examples of Low-Cost S&P 500 ETFs:

- Vanguard S&P 500 ETF (VOO): Expense ratio of 0.03%.
- SPDR S&P 500 ETF Trust (SPY): Known for high liquidity, with an expense ratio of 0.0945%.
- iShares Core S&P 500 ETF (IVV): Expense ratio of 0.03%, offering broad market participation.

Summary: Investing in low-cost ETFs, especially those tracking the S&P 500, provides a simple and cost-effective way to capture the overall performance of the U.S. stock market. With historical long-term returns averaging around 10%, these ETFs are appealing for building wealth over time. By embracing a long-term mindset and understanding the power of compounding, you can take advantage of this reliable strategy for financial growth and security.

YOUR MONEY

If the details above feel complex, here's the key takeaway: **Long-term growth through compounding**. Let's revisit this essential concept.

Long-Term Growth: Compounding returns can significantly grow wealth over decades. With an average 10% annual return, your investment could double approximately every seven years. The S&P 500, for instance, has historically averaged around this return rate over long periods.

The strategy is simple: **Invest consistently and think long-term.** Committing to a low-risk, compounding strategy like the S&P 500 allows your money to grow steadily over time. Investing is not a short-term fix but a pathway to true financial transformation. Patience and consistency are crucial, as this approach is most effective over decades, not years or months

Warren Buffett, the world's leading investor, was asked, 'Your investment strategy is so simple; why don't more people do it?' Buffet replied, '**No one likes getting rich slowly**.'

Consider investing monthly from now on to maximise long-term growth. The more you invest regularly, the greater your returns will be in the long run. In the U.K., investments up to £20,000 per year are tax-free, so take full advantage of this allowance.

An example table of potential returns at a 10% compounded growth rate over decades shows how long-term investing and patience can lead to substantial growth.

Investment growth over time

Monthly Investment	Future Value 10 years	20 years	30 years	40 years
£50	£10,327	£38,284	£112,966	£318,839
£100	£20,655	£76,569	£227,832	£637,678
£250	£51,638	£191,424	£569,831	£1,594,195
£500	£103,276	£382,848	£1,139,662	£3,188,390
£1,000	£206,552	£765,696	£2,279,325	£6,376,780

This strategy is accessible to everyone—start now, stay consistent, and let time do the rest.

Tax-Free Investment Vehicles in the U.K.

The U.K. offers several tax-free investment options that significantly benefit long-term financial growth. Below are key vehicles for U.K. residents:

1. Stocks and Shares ISA

- **Description**: A tax-efficient investment account allows individuals to invest in various assets, such as stocks, bonds, and mutual funds.
- **Key Benefits**:
    - **Tax-Free Growth**: No Income Tax or Capital Gains Tax on earnings, dividends, or interest within the ISA.
    - **Annual Allowance**: For the 2023/24 tax year, individuals can invest up to £20,000 across all ISAs (including Stocks and Shares ISAs, Cash ISAs, and others).
    - **Investment Flexibility**: Options range from individual stocks to index funds and managed portfolios, allowing investors to align investments with their risk tolerance and financial goals.
    - **Withdrawals and Transfers**: Funds can be withdrawn without penalty. However, once withdrawn, they cannot

be re-added within the same tax year if the annual allowance has been maximised. Transfers between ISA types are permitted, preserving the tax-free status.

2. Lifetime ISA (LISA)

- **Description**: A savings vehicle for first-time home buyers or retirement savings, available to individuals aged 18-39.
- **Key Benefits**:
    - **Government Bonus**: The government adds a 25% bonus to contributions up to £4,000 annually, which equates to up to £1,000 per year in bonus funds.
    - **Tax-Free Growth**: Like other ISAs, LISAs grow without Income Tax or Capital Gains Tax.
    - **Usage Restrictions**: Funds can be used to purchase a first home or withdraw after age 60 without penalties. Early withdrawals for other purposes may incur a penalty.

3. Junior ISA (JISA)

- **Description**: A tax-free savings account for children under 18, providing a head start on saving for their future.
- **Key Benefits**:
- **Annual Allowance**: Up to £9,000 can be contributed to the 2023/24 tax year.
- **Tax-Free Growth**: Investments grow free from Income Tax and Capital Gains Tax.
- **Access**: Funds are locked until the child turns 18 when the account is automatically converted into an adult ISA.

Why Choose Tax-Free Investment Vehicles?

- **Tax Efficiency**: These accounts provide opportunities to grow wealth without paying tax on the returns, maximising the effectiveness of your savings.
- **Long-Term Growth**: Investment ISAs, especially Stocks and Shares ISAs, offer the potential for higher returns compared to traditional savings accounts, making them ideal for long-term financial growth.
- **Flexibility**: The ability to choose between different types of assets allows individuals to tailor investments to their goals and risk tolerance.

Conclusion: For U.K. residents, taking advantage of tax-free investment vehicles like Stocks and Shares ISAs, Lifetime ISAs, and Junior ISAs is a strategic way to build wealth and achieve financial goals. By maximising annual allowances and investing consistently, individuals can grow their savings more effectively while enjoying significant tax benefits.

YOUR EXPENSES

Investing in Your Future: Rethinking Lifestyle Choices for Financial and Health Gains

Financial security and good health are the cornerstones of a fulfilling future. By reshaping your reward system and making intentional lifestyle choices, you can save money, enhance your well-being, and build long-term wealth.

Reflect on Your Spending

Take a moment to assess how much you've spent recently on non-essential items like:

- Alcohol
- Takeaways and dining out
- Sugar-laden and processed foods
- Smoking
- Recreational drugs
- Nights out
- Car payments
- Impulse purchases (e.g., gadgets, fashion, or video games)

Choosing Long-Term Gains Over Short-Term Pleasures

While indulgences like alcohol, takeaways, or smoking may offer short-term satisfaction, they often come at the expense of your health, financial stability, and independence. Each choice you make today influences your future self's well-being and freedom.

Cooking meals at home, for instance, isn't just cost-effective—it's an investment in better health. Processed foods create energy-draining cycles of cravings, while home-cooked meals promote vitality and financial freedom. Similarly, resisting the allure of must-have gadgets or costly car payments ensures your finances are directed toward lasting security rather than fleeting gratification.

Redefining Rewards

Skipping a night out doesn't mean missing out—it's a chance to redirect your time and money toward activities that nourish you, such as building skills, strengthening relationships, or enjoying restorative rest. These mindful decisions foster resilience and a sense of purpose, reinforcing your commitment to a brighter future.

Strategies for Healthier Choices and Financial Freedom

- **Cut Down on Alcohol**: Reducing or eliminating alcohol lowers both your expenses and calorie intake while improving overall health.
- **Cook at Home**: Home-cooked meals are healthier and more affordable. Reserve dining out for special occasions.
- **Limit Sugar and Processed Foods**: Choose whole foods to stabilise energy levels, improve mood, and save money in the long run.
- **Skip Recreational Drugs and Excessive Nights Out**: Focus on hobbies, quality time with loved ones, or restful nights that enhance mental clarity and well-being.
- **Avoid Costly Car Payments**: opt for a reliable, affordable car to free up funds for investments and experiences.
- **Resist Impulse Purchases**: Delay non-essential purchases to evaluate their true value, promoting better financial habits.

Small Choices, Big Impact

Every mindful choice you make today builds the foundation for a life of freedom, stability, and opportunity. The sacrifices you perceive now—such as skipping indulgences or prioritising savings—are investments in your future self's happiness and peace of mind.

Saving and Investing with Purpose

Approach saving and investing with clear goals that reflect your values. Whether it's financial independence, education for your children, or time to pursue passions, aligning your money with meaningful aspirations creates a purposeful life.

Key Areas to Prioritise:

- **Time and Freedom**: Save and invest now to enable early retirement, career shifts, or quality time with loved ones.
- **Children's Education**: Support your children's growth and success through education and resources.
- **Health and Wellness**: Prioritise preventive care, fitness, and mental well-being for a higher quality of life.
- **Purposeful Retirement**: Plan a retirement filled with meaningful pursuits such as volunteering, learning, or travel.
- **Experiences and Travel**: Invest in creating memories and gaining a broader perspective.
- **Entrepreneurial Dreams**: Fund passion projects or businesses that align with your values and contribute to others.
- **Philanthropy**: Save for charitable giving or community support, leaving a legacy of impact.
- **Family Support**: Build a financial safety net for loved ones, ageing parents, or grandchildren.

Intentional Living: A Richer Life

Material possessions lose significance as you age, while relationships and experiences take centre stage. Instead of fleeting pleasures, focus on creating a life of meaning and connection. A thoughtfully designed financial plan ensures you can enjoy a future where your time is yours.

Let's consider your monthly costs. Are there any areas where you could save £50 or £100 this month and put it towards your first investment? Please calculate your costs, write them down and see what opportunities are available.

In the future, what will matter the most to you? What would you do with it if you had 3 times more money in 15 years? How would it change your life?

Let's take some time to reflect and see how far we have come.

I believe in you.

A REFLECTION ON MONEY, TIME, AND CHOICES

Now that I am in my mid-40s, I've realised that while income is valuable, time truly matters, and money is a tool for securing freedom and choice. Though fortunate to have a good job and the potential to earn more, I can't reclaim the money I didn't use wisely in my earlier years.

One of my most significant financial decisions was buying my dream car in my early 30s—a BMW 6 Series convertible for £38,500. It felt like an achievement, a symbol of success, and it brought me joy every time I drove it.

Nine years later, I sold that car for £7,300. While I expected it to depreciate, I didn't realise by quite how much. My car lost 81% of its value.

When I consider 'why' I wanted my dream car and 'why' it was necessary, I realise that it was a statement to myself and the world of the success I had created. This is a need driven by external validation, seeking fulfilment outside myself.

If I'd invested that £38,500 in the S&P 500, it could have grown to £90,781 today.

When you have decisions to make, will you look for instant gratification or long-term gain? Wealth is quiet, not loud, remember.

When I bought that car, I was single. Today, I'm married with a family, and I've replaced the flashy car with a family-friendly one. I don't regret my choice, but I understand the trade-offs more clearly now.

The Power of Compounding and Long-Term Investing

Consider that £38,500 again:

- Over 20 years, at a 10% annual return, it could have grown to £259,009.
- Over 30 years, it could have reached around £671,802.

This perspective applies to any amount. A small expense today could grow exponentially over time. Investing with a long-term mindset and prioritising assets over liabilities builds a future of freedom and choice, not fleeting indulgences.

Micro-Savings and Their Long-Term Impact

Small, consistent savings grow significantly over time:

- £1,000 invested will 2x in 7 years = £2,000
- £1,000 invested will 4x in 14 years = £4,000
- £1,000 invested will 8x in 21 years = £8,000
- £1,000 invested will 16x in 28 years = £16,000

Starting small and early makes a substantial difference.

Starting an investment plan early for children can yield remarkable results over time. Imagine opening a tax-free investment account, such as a Junior ISA, and contributing £1,000 annually. With an average annual return of 10%, that investment could grow to approximately £442,593 over 40 years and reach around £1,163,909 over 50 years.

Teaching children the value of long-term investing over immediate spending can set them up for a lifetime of financial security and independence. Instilling these principles when children are young gives them a powerful tool for future growth that transcends short-term gratification. Investing in their future is not just about the money—it's about building a mindset that values patience, strategic thinking, and financial empowerment.

The Real Value of Money

After reflecting on the money I spent on cars, nights out, and an array of other unnecessary purchases, I now understand how much further I could have been today had I invested more purposefully.

True wealth is the quiet confidence of knowing you've built a foundation of security and freedom. Start small, stay consistent, and invest with a long-term view. Your future self—and your family's future—will be grateful for the choices you make today.

Remember, the best time to start investing was 20 years ago; the next best time is now. The valid reward lies not in what you spend today but, in the freedom, security, and opportunities you will gain from investing in your future.

What does this section on money mean for you? Can you journal and see how your mindset might have shifted from a short-term gain to considering your long-term financial stability?

CHAPTER 9
YOUR SOUL

A Moment of Reflection and Gratitude

Congratulations on making it this far in the book. I am honoured and inspired by your commitment to reading and, hopefully, taking action to transform your life. I have aimed to help you create a future that aligns your mind, body, money, and soul while healing the past and providing clear direction.

We began by addressing what it feels like to be lost—unsure of where life is headed and directionless. It's a common and challenging experience. Throughout these pages, I've shared lessons I wish I'd known in my twenties when I felt lost. I was driven by external validation and temporary highs: drinking, emotional eating, and impulsive decisions. Although I earned well, I lacked financial insight, leading to mistakes and missed opportunities that could have set me up for long-term financial stability and freedom.

This book is the guide I wish I'd had two decades ago, written for those who might see themselves in my past. While I don't regret my journey, better self-control and wiser choices would have spared me years of struggle. Having done the work to understand and grow, I can share these hard-earned insights to help you avoid the same pitfalls.

This book is about aligning your mindset, body, finances, and soul to build the life you desire thoughtfully and sustainably.

Laying the Foundation for Change

Building a solid mindset is crucial, so practices such as journaling, Meditation, regular movement, and mindful eating are essential. These consistent, small actions unravel the feeling of being lost and pave the way for clarity and self-discovery. They are the building blocks that help you move from just surviving to actively thriving.

If you review the ideas and diagrams shared earlier, you'll notice that feeling lost often stems from cycles of seeking temporary relief. By stepping away from these cycles, life begins to transform. Prioritising your mind, body, and financial health creates a solid platform for deeper exploration and discovering what truly matters to you.

A Path to Self-Actualisation

Now is the perfect time to reflect on what you truly want for your future.

My journey—from overcoming basic needs and breaking unhealthy cycles to reaching independence and fulfilment—has culminated in the growth and joy of writing this book. It represents moving beyond limitations and stepping into a life of learning, development, and play.

The question now is: what will you do with this newfound clarity? Take time to reflect, explore, and design the life you truly want. In the following sections, we'll look deeper into understanding your soul's desires. You don't need to have all the answers or make immediate plans. As your self-care routines improve and you move from surviving to thriving, your intuition will guide you. Your soul will communicate clearly, leading you towards an authentic life full of passion and excitement.

A Life of True Joy Awaits

Humans who live naturally thrive and feel great about life. This chapter encourages you to know yourself and listen to your inner voice. Soon, you'll find that the life you've always wanted—one filled with joy, purpose, and freedom—becomes a reality created by your choices and built on the foundation of your authentic self.

ANOTHER LOOK INTO MEDITATION

Revisiting the Power of Meditation

While Meditation was mentioned earlier in this book, I'd like to delve deeper into its value now that you can shape how you'll spend the rest of your life. Daily Meditation is not just a practice; it's a transformative habit that can create a foundation for mental clarity, emotional balance, and overall well-being.

Why Meditation Matters

Meditation trains the mind to focus, observe thoughts without judgment, and redirect attention when needed. It is a powerful tool for managing stress, improving emotional health, and fostering self-awareness. While it's often associated with spirituality, Meditation is accessible to anyone, regardless of beliefs, to cultivate inner peace and a deeper understanding of oneself.

Types of Meditation to Explore

There are various meditation styles, each offering unique benefits:

- **Mindfulness Meditation**: Brings attention to the present moment without judgment, cultivating awareness and acceptance.
- **Guided Meditation**: This technique uses verbal prompts or visualisation to lead the mind through a specific focus, aiding relaxation and mental imagery.
- **Mantra Meditation**: Involves repeating a sound or word to centre thoughts and promote focus.
- **Loving-Kindness Meditation**: Encourages compassion by fostering positive feelings toward oneself and others.

Exploring different styles helps identify what resonates most with you as you carve out your path forward.

Building a Consistent Practice Creating a conducive environment for Meditation is essential. Find a quiet space where you can sit comfortably with minimal distractions. Whether seated on a cushion or chair, a relaxed yet alert posture is preferred. Starting with short sessions of 5-10 minutes and gradually extending them can make Meditation easier to integrate into your daily life. Consistency, more than duration, builds a lasting habit.

Practical Techniques for Beginners A simple approach for beginners is breath-focused Meditation. Sit comfortably, close your eyes, and focus on the natural rhythm of your breath. When your mind wanders, gently return to the breath without judgment. This practice develops presence and reduces reactivity to daily stressors.

Overcoming Challenges Meditation can be challenging. Racing thoughts, restlessness, and difficulty staying focused are common but natural parts of the process. Patience and self-compassion are crucial. Using guided meditation apps or resources can help establish a routine and provide support through the initial stages.

Popular Meditation Apps to Consider

- **Aura**: Personalised meditations, stories, and coaching for mental health.
- **Calm**: Sessions for stress management and better sleep.
- **Headspace**: Beginner-friendly with a range of guided practices.
- **Insight Timer**: A vast library of free meditations on various topics.
- **Ten Percent Happier**: Practical meditations geared towards those new to mindfulness.

Deepening Your Practice As you grow more comfortable with Meditation, advanced techniques like visualisation, mantras, and body scanning can enrich the experience. These practices promote more profound relaxation and bodily awareness, fostering a stronger connection between mind, body, and soul.

The Profound Impact of Meditation With regular practice, Meditation cultivates emotional resilience and mental clarity. It empowers you to respond thoughtfully to challenges, maintain composure in difficult situations, and develop more mindful relationships. The benefits go beyond the minutes spent in Meditation, extending into all areas of life and influencing how you engage with the world.

For many, Meditation brings unexpected rewards. It can shift your perspective on consumption, reduce stress-driven behaviours, and inspire healthier habits. The long-term effects can be life-changing, leading to a more profound sense of fulfilment and peace.

A Life Guided by Inner Peace As you explore how to spend the rest of your life, consider incorporating Meditation as a cornerstone practice. Meditation can guide you, helping you listen to your inner wisdom and align your actions with your valid values. Meditation offers not just moments of peace but a pathway to a life enriched by presence, resilience, and clarity. Embrace this practice; it will become essential to living your most authentic and fulfilling life.

HOW TO MEDITATE

Beginner's Guide to Starting Meditation

Starting Meditation might seem intimidating, but it's simple and adaptable to any lifestyle. Follow these steps to build a meditation practice that fits your needs.

1. Find a Quiet Space. Choose a space where you won't be disturbed. It can be a quiet corner at home, a park bench, or your office during a break. The goal is to feel comfortable and relaxed.

2. Sit Comfortably: Sit comfortably on a chair, cushion, or the floor with your back straight but relaxed. Your hands can rest on your knees or in your lap. If sitting isn't suitable, lying down is an option—just be mindful of sleepiness.

3. Close Your Eyes or Soften Your Gaze. Please close your eyes to help minimise distractions or keep them open with a soft gaze on the spot a few feet before you.

4. Focus on Your Breath: Take a few deep breaths, then let your breathing return to its natural rhythm. Notice how the breath feels as it enters and leaves your body—the rise and fall of your chest or the sensation at the tip of your nose.

5. Notice Your Thoughts: Your mind will usually wander. When it does, gently acknowledge it without judgment and refocus on your breath. Think of it as training a puppy—patiently guiding your attention back each time it strays.

6. Start Small. Begin with 5 to 10 minutes. This short time frame helps build the habit without feeling daunting. Increase the duration as you grow more comfortable.

7. End with Gratitude When your timer goes off, take a moment to appreciate yourself for practising. Open your eyes slowly, stretch if needed, and ease into your day.

8. Consistent practice is more important than duration. Even if brief, daily practice helps establish the habit and unlocks Meditation's benefits over time.

Tips for Success

- **Guided Meditations**: Apps or videos provide step-by-step instructions and can help maintain focus.
- **Be Patient**: Meditation is a skill that improves with practice. Some days will be easier than others.
- **Explore Techniques**: Try different styles, such as mindfulness, body scans, or loving-kindness Meditation, to find what resonates with you.

By following these steps, you'll create a meditation practice that fosters calm, focus, and a deeper connection to yourself.

INTRODUCING IKIGAI

Finding Your Ikigai: A Path to Purpose and Fulfilment

Aligning your daily actions with your true self is vital to your soul's well-being. Each of us has unique gifts and strengths that, when nurtured, bring fulfilment and joy. One powerful framework for understanding and aligning these aspects is the Japanese concept of *Ikigai*, which means "a reason for being."

The Four Elements of Ikigai

Ikigai is the intersection of these four essential areas:

1. **What You Love (Passion and Mission)**: Activities that excite and energise you.
2. **What You Are Good At (Profession and Passion)**: Skills and strengths you excel in.
3. **What the World Needs (Mission and Vocation)**: Ways you can contribute meaningfully.
4. **What You Can Be Paid For (Profession and Vocation)**: Practical means financially sustaining yourself.

Ikigai lies where these elements overlap, balancing personal satisfaction, societal contribution, and financial sustainability. This harmony leads to a more meaningful, joyful life.

Breaking Down the Elements

- **Passion** is the intersection of what you love and are good at, bringing joy and a sense of competence.
- **Mission**: The overlap of what you love, and the world's needs gives you purpose beyond yourself.
- **Profession**: Where your skills align with market demand, enabling financial gain but potentially lacking fulfilment if disconnected from love and purpose.
- **Vocation**: Addressing a need and earning an income, but potentially needing more passion if it's just a job.

Applying Ikigai to Your Life

To explore your Ikigai, please can you journal and consider these questions

- *What do I love?* List activities and causes that bring joy and make you lose track of time.

- ▸ ***What am I good at?*** Identify your skills and strengths, both professional and personal.
- ▸ ***What does the world need?*** Reflect on societal or community needs where you can make a difference.
- ▸ ***What can I be paid for?*** Consider how your skills and passions can align with market opportunities.

Take your time, and through this process, you might be able to find your Ikigai.

Examples of Ikigai in Action

- ▸ **Teacher**: Loves teaching (passion and mission), skilled at it (profession), meets the need for education (mission), and earns a living doing it (vocation).
- ▸ **Artist**: Passionate about art, skilled at creating (profession), contributes to the world's beauty (mission), and can monetise their work (vocation).
- ▸ **Social Entrepreneur**: Solves social issues (mission), skilled in business (profession), meets global needs (mission), and earns through innovative solutions (vocation).

Conclusion Ikigai encourages a balanced approach to life that integrates passion, skill, purpose, and practicality. It offers a path to continual growth, fulfilment, and contribution, empowering you to live a life rich with meaning and direction. Finding and nurturing your Ikigai can align your life with what truly matters, bringing long-term satisfaction and joy to yourself and those around you.

YOUR MOTIVATION

Whatever we choose to do in life, achieving long-term success depends on understanding and harnessing the correct type of motivation. Broadly, motivation falls into two categories: extrinsic and intrinsic. Each plays a distinct role in driving our actions, and finding the right balance between them can lead to meaningful and lasting engagement in our pursuits.

Extrinsic motivation stems from external rewards or pressures. This type of motivation aligns with external factors like rewards, recognition, or avoiding negative consequences. When we're extrinsically motivated, we pursue an activity not necessarily for enjoyment but for its outcomes, such as earning a salary, receiving praise, or achieving high grades. Extrinsic motivation is often effective for prompting immediate action, especially for tasks that may not be enjoyable.

One significant advantage of extrinsic motivation is its ability to encourage people to complete necessary but not enjoyable tasks. External incentives like bonuses or recognition can effectively meet deadlines or increase productivity in work or school environments. However, a fundamental limitation is that people may lose interest in the activity once the external reward is removed, reducing their long-term engagement or satisfaction.

In contrast, intrinsic motivation is driven by internal satisfaction and personal enjoyment. People motivated intrinsically are drawn to activities because they find them fulfilling or meaningful, regardless of any outside rewards. Common examples include:

- Playing a sport purely for enjoyment.
- Pursuing a hobby out of passion.
- Engaging in personal challenges that foster growth.

Intrinsic motivation can sustain interest and commitment over the long term, even when no external rewards exist.

The primary strength of intrinsic motivation is its ability to fuel enduring engagement, creativity, and resilience. When intrinsically motivated individuals are more likely to persevere through difficulties, they find personal meaning and satisfaction in the activity. However, fostering intrinsic motivation can be challenging, particularly for tasks that do not naturally align with one's interests or passions. Unlike extrinsic motivators, intrinsic motivation may require an environment that supports autonomy, creativity, and a sense of purpose.

Extrinsic motivation remains helpful in achieving short-term goals or initiating action in areas where tasks may not be enjoyable or rewarding. For instance, bonuses, promotions, or recognition can encourage employees to meet specific targets in a workplace setting. However, overemphasis on extrinsic rewards can sometimes lead to a decline in intrinsic motivation, as individuals may rely solely on external incentives.

Striking a balance between extrinsic and intrinsic motivators can produce the best outcomes. By combining both approaches, individuals can maintain the momentum needed to complete necessary tasks (driven by external rewards) while developing a deeper connection to their activities through personal growth and satisfaction. For example, an employee might be motivated by a salary (extrinsic) but find joy in creative projects or meaningful connections with colleagues (intrinsic).

The most compelling motivation strategies often incorporate both types, creating an environment that uses extrinsic incentives to prompt initial action while cultivating intrinsic motivation through autonomy, opportunities for development, and aligning tasks with personal interests. For organisations and individuals, structuring goals to include both motivators helps sustain motivation, improve performance, and enhance overall well-being.

Understanding and balancing extrinsic and intrinsic motivation is essential for long-term success. When used effectively, extrinsic rewards can enhance intrinsic motivation, creating a powerful blend that fosters sustained engagement and overall satisfaction. With this balance, individuals are more likely to remain committed, achieve high performance, and find fulfilment in their pursuits.

What type of career would intrinsically motivate you to succeed in the long-term future? Please journal. Are there many options you are considering, or is there one thing that stands out?

When you wrote about your Ikigai previously, was that extrinsically motivated or intrinsically motivated? Please challenge yourself and ensure that while money is a motivator, it is not the sole motivation. I have shown that in the investment explanation, you can create wealth even with small investments, so financially, you are already in a strong place; please don't pursue a career simply for the money. We must find balance.

Considering 'why' you do things and 'what' you do is essential work; take your time. Remember, considering how you show up daily profoundly impacts your life and the people around you and will help you.

LAW OF ATTRACTION AND CONSISTENT ACTION

The Law of Attraction is a philosophy that suggests our thoughts, beliefs, and feelings have the power to shape our reality. It proposes that positive thoughts attract positive outcomes, while negative thoughts can invite unwanted results. This approach, which regards thoughts as forms of energy, encourages us to maintain a positive mindset to attract success across areas like health, finances, and relationships. However, combining it with consistent, daily action is essential to benefit from the Law of Attraction truly. Together, these elements create a powerful synergy for sustainable, long-term growth.

Core Principles of the Law of Attraction

Like Attracts Like

The foundational idea of the Law of Attraction is that similar energies attract. When cultivating positive thoughts and emotions, we align ourselves with energy, attracting positive experiences, people, and opportunities. Conversely, if we dwell on negativity, we may invite more of it into our lives. For instance, someone who constantly believes "I can achieve my goals" is more likely to notice and pursue opportunities. However, with daily, consistent action, this positive thinking is necessary to stay strong. Pairing this mindset with intentional steps—like networking or skill-building—transforms attraction into tangible progress.

Manifestation

Manifestation is turning thoughts into reality by focusing intently on your desires and believing they are achievable. This technique includes setting intentions, practising affirmations, and maintaining a clear vision of your goals. However, while visualising success is empowering, manifestation requires consistent action to bring dreams to life. For example, if you manifest a healthier body, envisioning yourself fit and vibrant is a good start. Still, daily exercise, balanced nutrition, and hydration make this vision a reality. The Law of Attraction provides clarity, and consistent actions create momentum.

Visualisation

Visualisation is a core practice in the Law of Attraction, where you imagine yourself having already achieved your goals. By picturing your desired outcomes, you create a blueprint aligning your thoughts and emotions with your ambitions. Visualisation prepares the mind for action, making it easier to stay focused and motivated. For instance, if you visualise yourself as a successful entrepreneur, you will likely feel more motivated to pursue networking opportunities, learn new skills, and take calculated risks. Regular visualisations and daily efforts toward your goals create a solid pathway to success.

Gratitude

Gratitude is essential in the Law of Attraction because it cultivates a mindset of abundance. By appreciating what you already have, you shift focus from lack to fulfilment, raising your "vibrational energy" and creating space for new opportunities. Keeping a gratitude journal, where you write down daily reflections, reinforces this practice. When combined with action, gratitude fuels resilience—an essential quality for progress. For example, someone grateful for their job may feel more inspired to work diligently, seek growth, and attract new career opportunities. Gratitude alone brings positivity; gratitude with effort brings progress.

Affirmations

Affirmations are positive statements that help reframe beliefs, instilling confidence and motivation. When you repeat phrases like "I am successful" or "I am capable," you train your mind to focus on self-empowering thoughts, reinforcing a positive mindset. However, affirmations work best when paired with action. For example, affirming "I am disciplined and focused" while consistently setting aside time daily to work on personal projects strengthens both mindset and productivity. This combination of mental reinforcement and action makes goals more attainable, turning affirmations into a blueprint for real change.

Letting Go

A crucial component of the Law of Attraction is learning to release attachment to specific outcomes. While setting intentions and visualising goals are essential, clinging too tightly to results can create resistance and limit your openness to unexpected opportunities. Trusting the process and allowing space for flexibility are key. For example, if you're working toward a new career, trust that the right path will emerge even if initial attempts don't go as planned. By letting go, you can remain adaptable, taking consistent steps toward your vision while being open to new and even better possibilities.

Techniques to Practice the Law of Attraction with Action

- **Vision boards** are effective. They allow you to represent your goals visually, reminding you of what you're working toward.
- **Journaling** allows you to write about your goals as if they have already been achieved, reinforcing belief in your success.
- **Daily actions** aligned with these goals turn intention into progress. For example, if your vision board includes fitness goals and consistent actions—like exercising daily or meal prepping—

reinforce your visualised outcome with measurable steps toward achievement.

Benefits of Combining the Law of Attraction with Consistent Action

The Law of Attraction leads to transformative results when paired with consistent effort. A positive mindset encourages resilience, helping you navigate obstacles with optimism. Setting clear intentions can focus your energy, while daily actions provide the practical steps necessary to reach those goals. For example, someone manifesting financial stability might set an intention for wealth and prosperity. Still, their commitment to budgeting, investing, or developing new income streams brings this goal to fruition. Combining mindset with actionable steps ensures a steady path toward your dreams.

The Balanced Approach to Success

While the Law of Attraction can be powerful, balancing it with tangible, realistic steps is essential. Visualising success and practising gratitude lay a strong foundation, but acting creates the structure needed to reach your goals. Whether the goal is financial, relational, or personal, daily actions make abstract dreams achievable. The Law of Attraction fuels motivation, while consistent effort moves you toward your aspirations. This balance between belief and action leads to sustainable, fulfilling success in every area of life.

How can you incorporate the Law of Attraction and consistent daily actions into building the life you want? Journal daily on progress, create a vision board, and use visualisation techniques to play it out in your mind and bring it into reality.

421 Method of Law of Attraction

I would like to share the 421 method of the Law of Attraction, a beautiful and heart-centred practice for daily positive energy and manifestation.

The 421 Method

4 Thank You's:

Each day, express gratitude for four things in your life. These could be simple, everyday blessings or significant moments. This practice raises your vibration and sets a positive tone for the day by focusing on what you already appreciate.

2 Acts of Sending Love:

Take a moment to mentally send love and positive energy to two people who need it. This could be friends, family members, or even strangers going through tough times. This act fosters compassion, connection, and energy of giving, contributing to your well-being and aligning you with positive vibrations.

1 Wish:

Make one wish or set one intention for yourself. This wish could relate to personal goals, well-being, or any desire you want to manifest. By doing this daily, you will keep your focus on your intentions and allow your subconscious to align with them.

How to Practice It:

- **Morning Routine**: Incorporate this practice into your morning ritual to start your day with positivity and intention.
- **Evening Reflection**: You could also do this in the evening to reflect on the day with gratitude, love, and hope for the future.
- **Write It Down**: Journaling these practices can deepen their impact, help you stay committed, and track how they evolve over time.

Benefits:

- **Boosts Positivity**: Gratitude and love elevate your mood and create a more positive outlook.
- **Strengthens Connections**: Mentally sending love helps maintain compassion and empathy toward others.
- **Clarifies Intentions**: Setting one daily wish keeps your goals and desires at the forefront of your mind, making manifestation more focused and intentional.

This simple yet profound daily routine can help align your energy with abundance and cultivate peace and purpose.

10,000 HOURS TO BECOME A MASTER

The **10,000-Hour Rule** suggests that mastery in any field requires a minimum of 10,000 hours of dedicated practice. This concept, popularised by author Malcolm Gladwell in his book *Outliers*, is based on research by psychologist Anders Ericsson, who studied the factors differentiating experts from novices. According to this rule, to truly excel and be recognised as an expert in an area—music, sports, science, or art—a person needs to invest significant time and effort in practising and refining their skills.

At its core, the 10,000-Hour Rule emphasises that **consistent, deliberate practice** is more critical to becoming an expert than innate talent alone. Ericsson's research demonstrated that high achievers spent thousands of hours in focused practice, often working under expert guidance and breaking down their learning into smaller, targeted challenges. This type of practice builds expertise by reinforcing skills, reducing errors, and improving one's ability to perform under pressure.

However, not just any practice counts towards mastery. The **quality of practice** is as vital as the quantity. Deliberate practice involves setting specific goals, focusing intensely, and receiving regular feedback to adjust. For example, a musician working on perfecting a challenging piece doesn't just play it from beginning to end; they identify difficult sections, work through them slowly, and repeat until they achieve precision. This focused approach is what propels learning forward effectively.

The 10,000-Hour Rule resonates because it frames expertise as **attainable through persistence and effort** rather than something reserved for the naturally gifted. It suggests that anyone can improve if they're willing to dedicate time and energy. For example, athletes like Serena Williams and musicians like Mozart weren't born masters; they each committed years of practice from a young age to build their skills.

This summary is encouraging for those passionate about a field and willing to invest the time to grow.

However, the 10,000-hour rule has limitations, particularly regarding **individual differences** and the influence of natural aptitude. Some people may reach high proficiency levels before the 10,000-hour mark, while others may need even more time to achieve mastery. The rule is, therefore, best understood as a general guideline rather than an exact formula. Motivation, access to resources, and personal resilience also play a role in achieving expert-level skills.

Critics of the rule argue that focusing solely on hours might lead to burnout or disillusionment if mastery appears differently than expected. They suggest balancing deliberate practice with rest and adaptability, ensuring the journey towards expertise remains sustainable and fulfilling. This perspective underscores the importance of enjoying the process rather than fixating only on reaching a target number of hours.

Why people become good at their jobs

If someone has worked a particular job, such as a software engineer, for 20 years. If they work an average of 40 hours per week, considering standard holidays and weekends, here's an approximate calculation of their hours of experience:

1. **Weekly Hours**: 40 hours per week
2. **Annual Weeks Worked**: Assume around 48 weeks per year (allowing for holidays and time off)

40 hours x 48 weeks x 20 years = 1920 hours per year
X 5 years = 9,600 hours

X 10 years = 19,200 hours
X 20 years = 38,400 hours

In this example, a person would accumulate **38,400 hours** over 20 years in the role, far surpassing the 10,000-hour mark. This extended experience allows them to refine their skills, handle complex problems, and anticipate challenges intuitively.

In addition, seasoned professionals benefit from **accumulated knowledge** developed through exposure to various scenarios, challenges, and industry changes. This depth of experience often enables them to mentor others, lead projects, and make high-level strategic decisions, solidifying their expertise.

In summary, the 10,000-Hour Rule offers a powerful message about the value of commitment, resilience, and focused effort in achieving mastery. While not an absolute, it is a valuable benchmark, encouraging us to recognise that real expertise comes from dedication over time. It reminds us that we have the potential to reach impressive levels of skill, provided we are willing to put in the effort and engage deeply with the practice.

Sharing this with you is to set your expectations on the time expectancy to become great at something. When choosing which direction is your authentic self, you need to invest the hours to become great at it; working in the shadows for a few years is to be expected.

I am making the point that intrinsic motivation is essential. The years you spend learning and becoming a master must be enjoyable because you will spend the rest of your life practising and refining your skills. My message is to choose wisely around what truly and deeply intrinsically motivates you.

/// YOUR SOUL

PURPOSE, PASSION OR YOUR LIFE'S TASK

Finding what you're truly meant to do—your life's task—goes far beyond choosing a career or following societal expectations. It's about unearthing what resonates deep within, brings you alive, and fills you with a sense of meaning. The journey to discover your purpose isn't always straightforward; it requires introspection, patience, and, often, a willingness to challenge your current life. Pursuing purpose is to commit to wholeheartedly understanding who you are at your core, what you value most, and what you're willing to dedicate yourself towards; this is far beyond money; it's in your soul.

For many, discovering this life's task means searching for a passion that feels so natural and fulfilling that they're willing to invest the famous 10,000 hours to master it. Whether that task involves art, teaching, science, or something as specific as mentoring others, it should connect to something in your soul that feels indispensable. Passion is like a fire that fuels this journey, making the hard work feel worthwhile and the setbacks part of a larger narrative. This dedication goes beyond fleeting interests; it is a deep-seated drive to grow, learn, and create lasting impact. Reflecting on what you love doing—not for validation, money, or praise, but purely because it brings you joy—can often reveal clues to this purpose.

To find what resonates, you must be willing to dig deep and reflect on what you want and value most. Ask yourself what pursuits or activities make you lose track of time, what topics or challenges you return to, and what values lie at the heart of your actions. Sometimes, finding purpose requires reconnecting with parts of yourself buried under obligations or expectations. For instance, if you've always been drawn to storytelling but set it aside for a more "practical" path, revisiting that passion could reignite something essential within you. Purpose often lies in the intersection of our innate interests and the skills we feel compelled to cultivate.

Pursuing your life's task means being prepared for the long haul, as mastery takes time, energy, and commitment. The 10,000-hour rule serves as a reminder that becoming an expert or achieving fulfilment in any domain isn't an overnight journey. It's about showing up day after day, even when progress feels slow or invisible. Those hours demand patience and resilience and build confidence, skill, and insight. This investment is an act of self-respect, a declaration that you value your growth enough to dedicate yourself fully to it.

For some, the most challenging part may be letting go of external validation or societal pressures that push us toward specific paths. Discovering your life's purpose might mean deviating from what others expect of you or even taking risks that could lead to failure. However, following this more profound calling often brings a sense of fulfilment and freedom that success in other areas might not. Many who embark on this journey feel a profound shift as they align their lives more closely with what they genuinely love and believe in. Pursuing your purpose authentically, despite any challenges, leads to a life that feels true to who you are.

Once you connect with your purpose, commitment to mastery becomes a source of joy rather than obligation. Mastery doesn't mean reaching a destination but committing to continual improvement and refinement. Even after you've put in 10,000 hours, there's always more to learn and more ways to evolve. This mindset can keep you engaged forever, transforming work into a meaningful practice rather than a routine or a chore. True mastery combines knowledge with curiosity; each new skill level opens doors to deeper understanding.

Along this path, there will be moments when doubt creeps in or progress stalls. At these times, return to the reasons you started and what drives you. Remember that purpose isn't about achieving perfection but about dedicating yourself to something meaningful and fulfilling. The journey is an expression of your values and a testament to your belief in your potential. This resilience, built through years of practice, deepens your connection to the work, reinforcing a sense of meaning that endures.

Ultimately, finding and fulfilling your life's task is one of the most incredible journeys you can undertake. It is a path that connects you to yourself, challenges you to grow, and allows you to make a unique impact on the world. Pursuing mastery in something that resonates at your core creates a life rich with purpose and contentment, one where each day contributes to a legacy built on passion and commitment. This lifelong pursuit doesn't just shape what you do—it shapes who you become, transforming each challenge and achievement into a celebration of your true self.

How has this section on Your Soul helped shape your thinking for your future? Please journal. What has changed, or what have you learned about yourself?

What are you going to do differently moving forward? How can this moment in your life allow you to transform into the best version of yourself?

I am proud of you. We have come so far, and the great news is that this is just the beginning.

TRANSCENDENCE: EXPANDING MASLOW S VISION

Recognising Maslow's Vision of Self-Transcendence

In the latter stages of his career, Abraham Maslow revisited his famous hierarchy of needs to include a critical, final stage: **self-transcendence**. This addition elevates human fulfilment beyond self-actualisation—shifting from personal achievement to connecting with a greater purpose, whether through serving others, embracing spirituality, or contributing to the collective good. Maslow believed this expanded hierarchy provided a more holistic understanding of human motivation, where the ultimate satisfaction comes from transcending the self to engage with something more significant.

Self-transcendence is a personal and outward-facing journey. It requires individuals to move beyond ego-driven goals and focus instead on **shared humanity and universal values**.

This shift fosters a more profound sense of meaning as fulfilment becomes rooted in one's achievements, impact on the world, and connections cultivated with others.

Pyramid Diagram

SELF-TRANSCENDENCE
Orienting Goals & Motivations Beyond the Self

◉ **PEAK EXPERIENCE**

SELF-ACTUALIZATION
One's Fullest Potential

SELF-ESTEEM
Accomplishment & Mastery

LOVE & BELONGING
Community, Family, Romance

SAFETY
Feelings of Security & Stability

PHYSIOLOGICAL NEEDS
Food, Water, Shelter, Warmth, Rest

The Essence of Self-Transcendence

Self-transcendence is about expanding beyond self-interest to embrace contributions, connections, and causes that extend beyond personal gratification. Unlike self-actualisation, which centres on individual potential, self-transcendence focuses on shared growth and collective well-being. It challenges individuals to dissolve boundaries between the self and others, fostering a profound sense of interconnectedness.

Maslow's concept offers practical and philosophical insights into this transformative state. From creative expression to spiritual exploration and acts of kindness, self-transcendence encourages intentional living that aligns personal actions with larger purposes. Individuals unlock higher levels of empathy, meaning, and fulfilment by transcending self-centred motivations.

Practical Steps to Cultivate Self-Transcendence

1. **Engage in Acts of Kindness**: Extend your focus beyond personal concerns by volunteering, mentoring, or supporting others in need. Simple acts like helping a neighbour or contributing to a community project foster a sense of purpose and interconnectedness.
2. **Express Creativity**: Use creative outlets—writing, painting, music, or other forms of expression—to connect with others through shared ideas and emotions. Creativity transforms personal experiences into something meaningful for a wider audience.
3. **Embrace Mindfulness**: Incorporate mindfulness practices, such as meditation or reflective journaling, into daily life. These moments create space to explore inner values and connect with a greater sense of being.
4. **Foster Gratitude**: Reflect on what you appreciate about your life and the world around you. Gratitude shifts focus away from scarcity and self-interest, nurturing a positive and outward-facing mindset.

Overcoming Challenges on the Path to Transcendence

The journey to self-transcendence is not without obstacles. Cultural norms prioritising individual success or societal expectations discouraging vulnerability can act as barriers.

Similarly, personal fears—such as stepping outside one's comfort zone or confronting change—may hinder progress.

To navigate these challenges, cultivate awareness of limiting beliefs, practice self-compassion, and seek supportive communities aligned with your values. Gradual steps, such as introducing small acts of kindness or exploring mindfulness, can help dismantle resistance and encourage steady growth toward transcendence.

Personal Growth Through Self-Transcendence

Self-transcendence fosters profound personal growth by challenging individuals to explore beyond their perceived limitations. In seeking meaningful contributions to the collective good, people often surpass self-imposed barriers, unlocking resilience, creativity, and newfound purpose. This journey transforms life into discovery, fulfilment, and limitless potential.

Connection and Contribution

At its core, self-transcendence nurtures empathy and fosters deeper connections. It enables individuals to see life through others' perspectives, creating a foundation for inclusivity and understanding. Acts of service and shared purpose contribute to societal harmony, bridging divides and promoting progress.

Collective self-transcendence drives positive change on a broader scale. When communities embrace shared values and prioritise mutual well-being, they lay the groundwork for meaningful advancements in equality, education, and sustainability.

Living a Transcendent Life

Maslow's concept of self-transcendence is not a distant ideal but an achievable way of life. It invites individuals to integrate its principles into everyday routines—cultivating empathy, expressing creativity, and aligning personal actions with higher purposes. By doing so, life becomes a tapestry of meaningful moments, where each choice reflects a commitment to personal and collective growth.

In practising self-transcendence, individuals create a legacy of fulfilment and connection. As Maslow envisioned, humanity's greatest potential lies not in isolation but in its capacity to uplift and transform the world through unity, compassion, and shared purpose. Embracing self-transcendence enriches not only individual lives but also humanity's collective future.

HELP WHO YOU WERE

Living a Transcendent Life: A Call to Action

Living a transcendent life is not about perfection. It's about transformation—taking the pain, confusion, and struggles you once endured and using them to create something meaningful for others. Transcendence begins when you recognise that your journey, with all its imperfections and triumphs, is the very tool that can inspire and guide others. This is about _helping who you were_.

Take my journey, for instance. I was once lost, confused, and broken, wrestling with inner conflicts and a never-ending stream of challenges. Over two decades, I acquired the knowledge, tools, and resilience to rise above it. Today, my purpose is clear: to share that knowledge with you. To help you rise, heal, and grow. That is my transcendence—using my past to guide you to a better future. This book is my legacy, a reflection of transcendence in action and an invitation to embrace your own.

Turning Pain into Purpose

Let's take a practical example. Imagine you're someone who feels stuck in your life, perhaps struggling with obesity. Your weight is more than physical—it culminates years of hardship, unmet needs, and societal pressures. Recognising this isn't about blame; it's about understanding. But now, imagine flipping the script. What if this pain becomes the foundation of your purpose?

You start your journey of change, one small step at a time. Perhaps you document it—sharing your highs, lows, breakthroughs, and setbacks. Vulnerability becomes your superpower, and your honesty resonates with countless others who see themselves in your story. Over time, as your health transforms, you become a beacon of hope. One day, you realise your journey has changed your life and inspired millions of others to begin their own. You've transcended—shedding the weight and helping countless others do the same.

Helping Who You Were

Now, let's shift to another scenario: a person battling alcohol addiction. Your struggle is overwhelming, and the path to sobriety feels impossible. But what if today, in this moment, you decide that his pain will no longer define you? You begin your journey toward recovery. You reach out for help, seek support, and learn how to reclaim your life. And you gain strength; you start to share your story.

You connect with others trapped in the same cycle through your vulnerability and courage. You offer them hope, tools, and encouragement. You become a voice for change, saving yourself and contributing to the lives of millions. In a world where three million people die annually from alcohol-related causes, your transcendence becomes a ripple that sparks transformation for many.

From Vulnerability to Influence

The beauty of transcendence is its accessibility in the modern world. You don't need perfection, wealth, or elaborate resources to begin. You just need your story and the courage to share it. In this digital age, your phone can be your platform, and your voice is your most powerful tool. Whether through a blog, a podcast, or social media, your journey can reach and inspire millions.

Imagine becoming the person you needed when struggling—the guide, the friend, the light in the darkness. By helping who you were, you create a legacy that uplifts yourself and countless others. Your story doesn't just heal you; it becomes the catalyst for healing others.

The Power of Transcendence

Transcendence isn't reserved for the extraordinary. It's a choice available to every person. It's about taking responsibility for your growth and using your transformation to elevate others. It's about acknowledging your pain and seeing it as the seed for something more significant—a way to inspire, connect, and lead.

So, what's your story? What challenges have shaped you? What lessons can you offer those walking a path you've already travelled? Begin there. Start small, but start now. Your journey is not insignificant. It can change lives—not just your own but those waiting for the inspiration you can offer.

Your Opportunity to Rise

This is your moment. The trials you've endured, battles you've fought, and victories you've earned all serve a purpose. You are living proof that change is possible, that growth is real, and that transformation is worth it. So, take the first step. Share your story. Be vulnerable, be authentic, and let your journey guide others toward hope, healing, and transcendence.

Remember: transcendence is not about leaving your past behind—it's about transforming it into something that serves the greater good. Help who you were. In doing so, you'll live a transcendent life and create a ripple effect of positivity and purpose that echoes far beyond your own existence.

THE FINAL CHAPTER
YOUR ESCAPE

This is it. It's your moment to take control and create the life you've always wanted. I'm asking you to commit to 120 days—one day at a time—to completely transform into the healthiest, most mindful, and most authentic version of yourself. These four months will redefine your potential and lay the foundation for a life of purpose, clarity, and strength. The time is now. No more waiting. No more excuses.

Over the next 120 days, you'll stop consuming the things that hold you back—sugar, alcohol, processed foods, and any other toxic habits. Instead, you'll fuel your body with real, nourishing food: fruits, vegetables, lean proteins, and whole grains. You'll walk daily, journal, meditate, and connect with the inner voice you've silenced for far too long. This isn't just a diet or a challenge—it's a full reset of your physical, emotional, and mental well-being. Every step you take will bring you closer to the person you've always known you could be.

Yes, it will be challenging. Cravings for alcohol, sugar, or other substances may arise in the first few weeks, maybe even months. These urges will test you, but they are temporary. When the "alcohol monster" or "sugar monster" arises, confront it with a simple, powerful thought: "_This won't help._" Because it won't, eating junk food or drinking alcohol will take you further away from your goals, your dreams, and your transcendence. Instead of giving in, replace the craving with action—take a walk, journal your thoughts, meditate, or even drink water. Cravings fade. Your goals endure. The better version of you is waiting, just beyond that urge.

/// YOUR ESCAPE

Here's the truth: the person you've always wanted to be is already within you. Your vibrant, authentic self is not a distant dream—it's a part of you that's ready to emerge. Over the next 120 days, you'll reconnect with your core values, rediscover your purpose, and finally let go of the toxic habits that have numbed your potential. This is your moment to listen to the voice inside that says, *"You're capable of so much more."*

The benefits of this journey will surprise you in ways you can't yet imagine. The fat will melt away, your energy will soar, and your mind will clear. As you stop spending money on alcohol, takeaways, and processed foods, you'll watch your savings grow. Every pound you save is an investment in the life you deserve—whether funding a dream, creating financial freedom, or simply enjoying the peace of living within your means.

At the end of these 120 days, you'll see someone transformed in the mirror. You'll feel proud, strong, and alive. You'll have proven to yourself that you are enough and capable and hold the power to design the life you've always wanted. The old you, weighed down by doubt and distraction, will be a distant memory. In its place will stand someone you admire.

You, for the first time in your life.

This isn't forever—it's 120 days. Four months to give yourself the chance to become your best self. After that, you'll make intentional choices about how to move forward, free from addiction, self-doubt, and the habits that have held you back. This is your time to break free, outgrow the life you've been stuck in, and step into a future that excites you.

Start today. One day at a time. One choice at a time. This is your escape and your transformation. Document and share it openly and be proud of your growth. Believe in yourself, and I know you've got this. Let's go—your best self is waiting.

THANK YOU

Thank **you** for joining me on this transformative journey. From the first page, you've shown a commitment to uncovering your true self, breaking free from old patterns, and building a life aligned with your deepest values. I am genuinely proud of your dedication and courage in completing this journey.

The personal development journey hasn't just been about reading words—it's been about transformation, growth, and stepping closer to the life you've always wanted. Every step you've taken has been a testament to your strength and resilience. You've delved deep, confronted challenges, and embraced change with an open heart.

As you move forward, remember that the best version of you is always within reach. Each choice brings you closer to a purpose, peace, and joy-filled life. Let this be just the beginning of a lifetime of growth, guided by your inner wisdom and fuelled by the intentions you've set.

Thank you for trusting me to be a part of your journey. I'm incredibly proud of your progress and inspired by the path ahead of you. Continue to move forward with courage, grace, and self-belief. The future you've envisioned is waiting—to meet it.

With all my gratitude, love and respect, Simon x

READY TO TRANSFORM YOUR LIFE? JOIN THE ARE YOU LOST IN YOUR SHIT? TRANSFORMATION GROUP!

If you're ready to take the next step towards becoming the best version of yourself, this is your moment. The *Are You Lost in Your Shit* Transformation Group is designed to help you break free from what's holding you back and create a life filled with clarity, purpose, and strength.

This isn't just another group—it's a powerful movement for real, lasting change. Through expert guidance, practical strategies, and the support of a motivated community, you'll tackle the five pillars of transformation: **Your Mind, Your Body, Your Money, Your Soul, and Your Escape.**

Here's what you'll get:

- **Live Workshops** to learn actionable strategies.
- **Interactive Challenges** to apply what you've learned.
- **Exclusive Resources** to keep you on track.
- **Accountability** and support from like-minded individuals on the same journey.

Say goodbye to self-doubt, bad habits, and feeling stuck. Together, we'll overcome the chaos and create the life you deserve. Transformation doesn't have to be lonely—join the group and experience the power of collective growth.

Your journey starts here. Let's take that next step together.

To check the group out, please go to **skool.com/areyoulostinyourshit**

Printed in Great Britain
by Amazon